IF IT WASN'T FOR THE CUSTOMERS
I'D REALLY LIKE THIS JOB

Stop Angry, Hostile Customers COLD While Remaining
Professional, Stress Free, Efficient, and Cool As A Cucumber.

BY

Robert Bacal, M.A.

BACAL & ASSOCIATES
722 St. Isidore Rd.
Casselman, Ontario, Canada, K0A 1M0
(613) 764-0241

This book is available in printed form, in Adobe Acrobat format, and in other electronic formats that can be read on smartphones, e-readers, Ipad and the Kindle.

We offer significant discounts for bulk purchases. To order multiple copies please contact us via e-mail at ceo@work911.com. For electronic versions that can be downloaded immediately, please go to http://busylearners.com

ISBN-13: 978-1452803807
ISBN-10: 1452803803

Disclaimer:

While this book is intended to provide accurate and authoritative information regarding dealing with angry and difficult customers, it is sold with the understanding that neither the author or publisher is offering a professional service via this book. It you require professional advice on topics related to this book or the situations therein, please consult a qualified professional (e.g. psychologist, lawyer, law enforcement, security expert).

Other Books By Robert Bacal

Published By McGraw-Hill

Perfect Phrases for Customer Service: Hundreds of Tools, Techniques, and Scripts for Handling Any Situation

The Manager's Guide to Performance Reviews

Perfect Phrases for Performance Reviews : Hundreds of Ready-to-Use Phrases That Describe Your Employees' Performance

How To Manage Performance: 24 Lessons to Improving Performance

The Complete Book of Perfect Phrases Book for Effective Managers

Perfect Phrases for Setting Performance Goals : Hundreds of Ready-to-Use Goals for Any Performance Plan or Review

Perfect Phrases For Managing Your Small Business

Other Publishers

If It Wasn't For My Co-Workers I'd Get Along With Everyone At Work (Forthcoming)

Conflict Prevention In The Workplace - Using Cooperative Communication

A Critical Look At Performance Management Systems - Why Don't They Work

Defusing Hostile/Volatile Situations For Educators (In Development)

Complete Idiots' Guide To Consulting (Out of Print)

Complete Idiots' Guide To Dealing With Difficult People (Out of Print)

Table of Content

Chapter I—Introduction

Chapter II — Understanding Hostile Behavior

Chapter III — Where Does Hostile and Abusive Behavior Come From?

Chapter IV — The Defusing Process and The CARP System

Chapter V — The Art of Self Control

Chapter VI — Starting Off Successfully

Chapter VII — The Art of Cooperative Language

Chapter VIII - Verbal Self-Defense Techniques

Chapter IX—Acknowledgment Techniques

Chapter X—Countering Non-Verbal Intimidation

Chapter XI—Referral Techniques

Chapter XII—Time Out! Disengaging

Chapter XIII—Problem Solving

Chapter XIV—Assertive Limit Setting

Chapter XV—For Managers and Supervisors

Chapter XVI — Customer Interactions Through Media

Chapter XVII — Audiences, Groups, Crowds and Mobs

Chapter XVIII—Special Topics

Chapter XIX — Final Comments

Chapter I

Introduction—The Customers That You Can't Get Out of Your Head

It just doesn't matter where you are employed, or the type of business. If you work in a library, or a shoe store, or a lawyer's office, you have met the customer you can't get out of your head. Work in the hospitality industry — hotels and restaurants? There they are. He, or she, since gender has nothing to do with politeness, is the person who is so annoying, rude, unreasonable, demeaning, impatient, and even threatening, that it's hard to get the person out of your head even after the encounter is long finished.

You wonder. What should have I said? Or, you berate yourself for not "not standing up for yourself" or being too slow to deliver the "killing" verbal insult that would put the offensive person in his or her place. You might even rant and rave about the person on the way home from work, and at the dinner table. Even worse, when the lights go out for the day, and you should be slipping into peaceful slumber, you lie there thinking about how unfair or vicious the customer was. Ouch.

You've rented space in your head, to a person who is going to make holes in the walls, and renege on the monthly rent. This head renting freeloader is never going to pay your "stress" bill.

You can legitimately say: <u>If it wasn't for the customers, I'd really like my job.</u> Which, not coincidentally is the title of this book.

This book will help you deal with these customers in a constructive and helpful way that will benefit you in the following ways, provided you use the techniques consistently and properly.

You will:

- Shorten the length of time you have to spend with angry, hostile and abusive customers, whether they are in the right or in the wrong. **You save time**.
- **Reduce the intensity of the customer's anger** so that they are less likely to target you, insult you, or even attack you physically and at the same time, you will come across as helpful.
- **Feel confident** that you can and will control difficult customer interactions and reduce the feelings of confusion (not knowing what to do), and helplessness.
- Convey the impression to your boss and colleagues that you are really good at what you do and in, particular, at keeping your cool in tough circumstances. **That means, you are more promotable**.

- Enjoy the **satisfaction of helping people** who start out angry, and end up happy you have been able to help them — the satisfaction of having done an excellent job.
- Stop bringing nasty customers home with you (your spouse will be so pleased), and ensure they don't sneak into your bed at night (well, thought wise). Learn to put it away when it is time to put it away. **Reduce the stress**.

SURVEYING THE CUSTOMER SERVICE LANDSCAPE

So, what is happening out there in customer service land? Have people become more aggressive and nasty over the years? Are they more demanding than they used to be? Maybe employees such as yourself have experienced attitude shifts? Where does management fit in? Let's take a look at the landscape in which you work. Let's consider the three main "players" — Employers, customers, and employees.

 Wise Thoughts To Ponder

Strangers and Power:
Why do you allow almost complete strangers to ruin your day? Are people you may never see again, and who don't know you, THAT important? Customers ARE important, but not on a personal, emotional basis

LIP SERVICE TO CUSTOMER SERVICE + LACK OF INVESTMENT = FRUSTRATED CUSTOMERS

No doubt you've heard the litany repeated over and over again. It's all about customer service. You have to amaze the customer. You need to be faster than a speeding bullet. Go above and beyond the call of duty. You've heard many of the slogans trucked out by managers and executives, pundits and consultants.

In a sense they are right. In a world where it's hard to compete on price, the service offered to the customer becomes a critical aspect of whether the customer returns, or at least, so it would seem.

The problem is that while companies push their employees to be better and better through exhortations, they usually look at customer service as an overhead COST, rather than an investment. When budget decisions are made, what happens?

1. In retail, companies reduce the number of people on the floor so when it gets busy, it's impossible for floor staff to do their jobs and serve customers quickly. Stores get messy, items are mispriced or lacking prices.

2. In terms of customer support, companies replace personal service with automated service (such as call centers, use of social media, etc), with the outcome that customers end up having to wait longer to be served if they need help or have a problem.

3. The people who have the power and authority (supervisors, managers) to help customers and solve problems are often, themselves overworked, so it can take some time for them to respond to a customer's phone message or email. The "underlings" are not allowed to make decisions beyond basic workaday fixes. It's not uncommon for employees who need authorization from a manager to not be able to find one quickly.

The outcome is obvious. Customers end up more frustrated and ready to jump down the throats of anyone working for the company. Worse yet, most companies act in this manner so the customer feels trapped. Psychologically that is never good. Frustrated, trapped people tend to be much more aggressive.

The other outcome is that employees get frustrated too, since they are often asked to do things that are nigh near impossible when the customer flow increases past a particular level. That means employees are more volatile and impatient too.

OVERBLOWN UNREASONABLE CUSTOMER DESIRES FED BY COMPANIES + LOW EXPECTATIONS = HAIR TRIGGER CUSTOMER BEHAVIOR

One thing that has changed over the years is that customers want more from companies. For example, twenty five years ago it would be unheard of (and laughable) if a customer tried to return something to a Gumby's Hardware Store when the item was purchased at the GoGoMart. If you didn't have the receipt, you'd be told to go pound sand, perhaps politely, perhaps not so politely.

Nowadays customers try this fairly often, because they've been taught by the companies and corporations that if you whine and complain long enough and loud enough, you can get away with things like this.

While companies balk at investing in more staff and training them to be better at their jobs, they have become more lax about the one off kinds of exceptions customers ask for. Hence, customers have completely unreasonable desires, and corporations have fed them. While not the only reason for inflated customer wants, it's a powerful one.

That's not the whole story. While they want more, customers also expect the worst when they shop. They are primed to be angry because while they want to be treated like kings and queens, they know that for many things, it's not going to happen. Things will go wrong. This is often accurate, since shopping has become more and more difficult and annoying for many people, as they face the results of staff cutbacks. Incorrectly priced items, no prices, long lineups, items out of stock, failure to return calls promptly are the norm. We all experience them on a daily basis.

The combination of wanting unreasonable levels of service PLUS anticipating and preparing for poor service means customers are frustrated or prepared to be angry even as they cross the threshold of the establishment.

THEN THERE'S THE EMPLOYEE (IS THAT YOU?)

In your job and in your role as a customer contact, your own motivations and skills are going to vary from day to day. Your mood, your current life situation, your health, and even what you did last night affect your patience levels. If you have a "bad week", or "bad day" it seems like customers overly picky or nasty, when in fact, they are not being "abnormal". Your mood affects your perceptions.

If you are **lower down in the corporate or company food chain**, it's likely that one or more of the following describe your situation.

- You don't see the job as permanent, and plan to do greater things, career wise.
- You aren't being paid a big whack of money to provide customer service.
- You feel overworked and without the support you need to do your job.
- You haven't received adequate training in dealing with angry difficult customers.

If these apply to you, then it's no wonder that you get impatient with customers who are intentionally difficult, and even those that are unintentionally annoying. Just hang on a second, though and we'll get back to your situation.

If you are in a **professional type position** (e.g. a lawyer in a firm, accountant, software programmer or IT support person), you probably:

- Believe your role is to practice law, or do financial paperwork, or create great software, rather than cater to annoying or difficult customers.
- Have had virtually no training in customer service or worse, in how to deal with angry, and distressed customers and clients.
- Are expected to handle tough situations on your own, since you get paid a fairly healthy wage to do so.

 Bet You Didn't Know

Satisfaction—Can You Get Some?
The best reasons to provide excellent customer service are selfish. First, doing so makes a job more satisfying, and second, calming angry customers means less abuse, stress, and anger for you .

You aren't going to get much sympathy from most people lower down in the corporate food chain, let's face it. Most professionals go into their chosen fields because they like the kind of work (e.g. going to court, preparing tax documents, doing certain kinds of analysis) and not because they are eager to be "great customer service representatives". That doesn't change the fact that, to succeed, you need customers and the customer/people skills to keep them. You can't always slough off the responsibility for dealing with irate and nasty clientele to the folks at the bottom of the food chain.

If you are a supervisor, manager or executive, it's likely that you see yourself as:

- Needing to spend your time on "more important things" and not on dealing with angry or difficult customers.
- Expecting those lower down in the organization to handle and defuse difficult and hostile clientele so they never reach you.

- You probably have no training in how to deal effectively with hostile situations, even if you came from the "floor". You may, however, believe that by virtue of achieving a management position, you are better at it than you actually are.
- You haven't dealt regularly and directly with customers so you tend to be out of touch with what's going on between your staff and the customers. The tendency is to underestimate the frequency and severity of employee-customer clashes and difficulties.

IN A NUTSHELL

What are the implications? What does it all mean?

First, to answer the question about whether customers are more demanding. The answer is yes. Are they more apt to be aggressive than before? Yes. Have companies made strides in dealing with difficult and angry customers? No. Are managers prepared to work together with line employees to defuse and turn around interactions with upset, hostile and angry customers? No, not generally.

The landscape of customer service has become a much more difficult environment in which to work, and that applies to both line employees, supervisors and executives. Generally, companies have not provided employees with the skills and guidance to handle tough customer situations effectively.

The people who are most "out in the open", those who experience customer challenges most regularly, tend to be the lowest paid.

This boils down to impaired customer service, high levels of stress for front line staff who sometimes, literally, become part of a "firing line", increases physical risk, and increased potential for lost customers.

WHAT DO THESE INTERACTIONS LOOK LIKE AND FEEL LIKE?

What kind of difficult customer interactions are we talking about? What do they feel like? What happens? Let's take a quick tour.

It's break time at the bank. Marie and Jack, both tellers, sit sipping coffee in the break room. Jack looks at Marie's tired face, and notices she seems pale, and tired.

"Marie, what's up? You look exhausted."

Marie answers, *"I didn't get much sleep last night. You remember that big guy who came in here and yelled at me because his check bounced. I couldn't get what he said to me out of my head, I was so infuriated. I kept thinking of what I should have said to him, or what I could have said, but I really wished I'd just told him to F*** off. Anyway, I didn't get much sleep."*

 Bet You Didn't Know

Baby Rattles:
Angry customers tend to revert to childish, tantrum-like behavior. Believe it or not we all have this tendency although most aren't proud of it.

It's important not to respond in the complementary parent role, since it escalates the anger.

Look at Your Own Behavior As A Customer

Have you become less tolerant when YOU are the customer? Thinking about your own experiences as a customer can help you understand why they get upset.

Jack replied. *"I've wanted to do that too, but you know where that would lead. Probably get fired. I can't figure out some of these customers. They make mistakes, blame the bank, and then yell, scream, and insult us personally, like we intentionally messed up their accounts. You know, if it weren't for these customers, I'd really like my job."*

Meanwhile, just next door, at Obie's Deli, Jane stands behind her counter, taking food orders from a line-up of customers – customers anxious to get their food and make the most of their break time.

"Next", Jane says, and the next customer steps up and just stares at her. She doesn't say anything – just glares. *"Yes?"*

Jane says, *"What can I get you today?"* The customer looks ready to explode, face red, fists clenched. She reminds Jane of a frustrated four year old about to fling mashed carrots against the wall, but Jane keeps that thought to herself.

Finally the customer speaks. *"What the hell is wrong with you people? I don't know if you are stupid or what, but I came in yesterday and I asked for a sesame seed bagel with plain cream cheese. That's s*e*s*a*m*e seed, not poppy seed."* The customer spells it out letter by letter as if Jane is an idiot.

Jane says, *"Something was wrong with your order?"* *"Damn right. Don't you get it? You gave me a poppy seed bagel and it's not the first time. I know Obie, the owner of this dump and I'm getting on the phone, and if it's the last thing I do I'm going to get you fired. If you don't know the difference between poppy and sesame, you're just too stupid to work anywhere. You probably don't know who I am, but…"*

The customer goes on and on, and while she talks she looks back at the audience of other customers, like she's on stage. The other customers stare at their shoes, or stare at their watches, because all they want is to get their food and get out of there.

Jane freezes, like a deer in the headlights of an oncoming car. Not a clue what to say or what to do. Her hands shake a bit, as if she's been threatened physically, her body automatically pushes adrenaline through her – essence of the fight or flight reaction.

Over at the Kugel Manufacturing Company, there's a meeting going on. We see Jennifer, the Vice-President of Operations pacing from corner to corner in her oak paneled office, and Jack sitting in a chair.

Jennifer says, *"Jack, let me get this right. Yesterday you got a call from Bob telling you that he had to stop the assembly line because he didn't have the parts you promised, right?"* Jack nods. *"And you basically told him to get stuffed? He told me that you were unhelpful, rude and disrespectful, and you refused to rectify your mistake. That's not acceptable, Jack. Will you explain all this to me?"*

Jack responds. *"Jennifer, that's not what happened at all. Bob called me swearing and yelling, and threatened to come to my office and not leave until he got his parts. I tried to explain the source of the problem to him, but he didn't hear a word I said. I offered several solutions, but nothing was good enough. I don't think he even cared about the parts. He just wanted to wail into someone. I TRIED to resolve the problem. The next thing I know he's running to you. I don't need to be treated that way."*

The meeting continues for over half an hour but, for Jack, it seems like days.

IT'S ALL TOO FAMILIAR.

If you deal with customers, whether paying customers (external customers), or internal customers like Bob, you KNOW these situations. You've been there. You ARE the employee, Jack, or Jane, or Marie.

It doesn't matter what industry or business you work in. It could be a hotel, restaurant, lawyer's office, accounting practice, call center, or hospital or doctor's office. There's no sector where you won't find difficult, hostile and challenging customers.

Sometimes you can feel for the hostile, or angry customer. Things go wrong. Things take time. Mistakes get made. After all, you're not only an employee of some organization dealing with customers, but you are also a customer yourself. You can almost understand why someone treats you badly out of frustration. Almost.

Other times, you can't be sympathetic with a hostile customer or client because you know that nothing you've done, and nothing your company has done, is wrong. No mistakes on your part.

You also know that customers make mistakes, and sometimes try to blame you. They forget things, or don't read what they need to read. Some try to pull "fast ones". They expect miracles. When they don't get miracles, they strike out. Since you are handy and available at the time, they strike out at you. Handy for them, hellish for you.

Regardless of why the customer is angry, and regardless of who is "at fault", nobody deserves to be abused, yelled at, threatened or insulted. That you deserve to be free of these things doesn't make it so. People will still act badly.

Since you will encounter these situations, and you can't completely avoid them, what you CAN do is learn to handle them so they don't take up huge of amounts of time, stress you out, ruin your day, control your emotional well-being, and basically drive you nuts.

Consider some realities about difficult customer service interactions.

You do not control the broad factors that contribute to customer impatience and volatility. You can't change society, you can't change expectations, and you can't do anything but your best, often within a flawed company system, to meet those higher expectations.

The problem is that you still bear the everyday challenges of customer service in a difficult time.

You end up paying a price, particularly if you don't have all of the available defusing hostile customers techniques at your fingertips.

WHO PAYS THE PRICE? AND HOW?

Of course, companies that deal with hostile customers, and fail at it, pay a price. Angry customers go elsewhere. They consume valuable time for companies, particularly if they end up speaking to managers, then the district managers, vice-presidents, and so on. Time is money.

Angry and dissatisfied customers also tell their friends of their bad treatment, and it is much more costly to acquire a new customer than to keep a current one.

That's all true. But it's the employees (that's you, probably) on the "firing line" who have to deal with the stresses, great and small, resulting from contact with angry, frustrated customers. Those customers eat up YOUR time. They interfere with your ability to serve other customers who are also impatient. The more aggressive customers can be so upsetting to deal with that you take them home. You let them "rent space in your head" even after you leave work for the day.

You pay that price. It doesn't have to be that way. You can learn defusing skills so the price you pay is minimal, even when dealing with the most difficult customers.

YOU CAN DO SOMETHING ABOUT IT

It may seem you can do little to defuse the anger and hostility of customers, or even more importantly, have a positive effect on how they behave. Bad customer behavior seems to be set off by the smallest things, and above all, it seems unpredictable. The truth of the matter is different. You can do things to defuse anger and reduce abusive behavior. You can learn to act in ways that reduce this kind of behavior. You can learn to stop "throwing gasoline" on customer anger-fueled fires.

You might have to alter your perspective and attitude, and, it takes skill. It takes some work to learn the skills. Then again, it's not that hard and the payoffs for you can be huge.

This book is designed to help you learn the skills. Through the text and exercises you will learn to use over eighty inter-related techniques to prevent escalation, and save time and reduce stress that is associated with hostile clientele. No, you can't eliminate it. But you can make huge gains in reducing it, through your own behavior.

HINTS FOR USING THIS BOOK

This book is not about Psychology or Psycholinguistics but it is based upon those disciplines. Included is just enough "theory" for you to understand WHY the specific and practical techniques work with angry people. Understanding is important because YOU need to decide what techniques to use, and when and with whom. You also need to be able to decide when to change strategies with a particular client.

We recommend that you read all the chapters even if some of the content is targeted to people in positions other than yours. For example, there's a chapter written for supervisors and managers. If you aren't a supervisor, read it anyway. Part of defusing angry customers and increasing workplace security and safety involves working together, and getting on the same wavelength.

Similarly, if you are a supervisor, manager or executive, read the whole book so you can support and/or teach your staff to use the techniques properly.

CAUTION!

Don't Believe In Magic
There is no magic solution, no cookbook approach that works for every customer and every situation. That's why attitude, judgment and having multiple defusing tools in your toolbox are so important to your success.

Here are a few more suggestions to maximize your learning from this book.

- Limit how much you read in a single sitting. One or two chapters at a time should be your maximum. There are a lot of things to learn, and you need time to assimilate the meanings before you move on. Don't overload yourself.
- Once you have read your "portion", ask yourself this question: "<u>How can I apply what is in this portion to my work tomorrow (or next workday)?</u> Write down your answer, to reinforce your commitment to yourself to test out or practice the material in your real environment.
- Take a few minutes at the end of each work day <u>to evaluate</u> whether you actually did what you committed to do in #2. How did it work out? What was effective? What was not?

SPECIAL FEATURES TO HELP YOU LEARN

On many of the pages, you'll find helpful boxes that communicate important information to you. Pay attention to them as you read the main text. You can also use these boxes to refresh your memory about the content of page(s) or a chapter, should you want to go back. This way you may not need to reread everything if all you need is a quick refresher.

Different boxes contain different things, and look a bit different.

The Caution Box: In this box you'll find out about things you should NOT do related to handling angry and difficult customers. Learning to work effectively with upset clients involves ceasing to do the things that don't work, and replacing those ineffective actions with better ones. The Caution Box will help you with the first part. There's a miniature example to the right.

The Snapshot Box: Summaries of the most important points on the page(s) will appear in these boxes. You'll find definitions, key principles, and vital explanations appearing. To the right is a miniature version of the Snapshot Box.

Wise Thoughts To Ponder: Contains questions and issues to help you understand your own reactions to people, or other ideas to think about. These will help you examine your attitudes, behaviors and motivations.

The Bet You Didn't Know Box: Contains information relevant to angry people and customer service that you may not have heard before. Most suited for background material.

REPETITION AND FLEXIBILITY

You might notice there is some repetition of some of the concepts in various chapters. There are several reasons for this. First, some concepts fit in more than one place. Second, for people who prefer to read individual chapters out of sequence, it means that you won't miss ideas from other sections. Finally, when altering interpersonal skills, repetition is an important part of the learning process.

CAVEATS—READ THIS. IT IS IMPORTANT

No seminar or set of learning materials can tell you exactly what to do in each individual situation. We must be clear that each hostile situation is different, and that you must use your own judgment to determine what you ought to be doing and saying. There is NO magic solution, no cookbook approach that works each time. This book includes tactics and techniques you can use, but YOU must decide when and how to implement the techniques when the time comes. Only you can make those decisions when "on the firing line". Also, you can't memorize scripts and just recite them with customers, particularly angry ones. Customers can tell when you are talking to them as a human being, and when not.

You can get better at it, and reap the benefits. There are few things more satisfying than successfully dealing with an angry customer so he or she leaves relatively satisfied.

IMPORTANT NOTE ON SAFETY

It is important – very important, that you consider safety as a bottom line. Your safety and the safety of other staff, and customers are paramount. There will be times when it will be impossible to defuse someone, particularly if he or she is prone to violence or mental instability. You should always be concerned, but not paranoid, about safety, and do what is required to keep everyone safe. **Always err on the side of safety!**

FINAL NOTE

As an additional resource, you might consider visiting our web site, **The Customer Service Zone**. There you will find summaries of over 1,000 articles about all aspects of customer service, special guest articles on the topic, and from there, you can access an open discussion list where you can ask questions about customer service in general or dealing with hostile customers. The site is at:

http://customerservicezone.com

Chapter II — Understanding Hostile **Behavior**

Why They Do What They Do – Understanding Angry, Hostile and Abusive Customer Behavior

Think about some the difficult customers you have encountered.. What did they look like? What did they do? What unpleasant things did they say?

Here is an important question. What percentage of nasty customers you face are nasty ALL the time, to everyone in their lives? If that percentage is high, let's say 90%, it means that most hostile and abusive customers are that way because of personality traits they bring with them wherever they go. If that percentage is much lower, it means that angry, hostile and **abusive customer behavior is "situational"**. In other words, it's triggered by circumstances and situations.

CAUTION!

Not Personality
Don't attribute bad customer behavior to personality, since that's usually not the case. Doing so puts you into a powerless and helpless victim place.

If nasty customer behavior is a result of "personality", then we are in trouble because we can't "change the personalities of difficult or abusive customers. We'd all be helpless.

Luckily, **nasty customer behavior isn't a result of "personality"**. The percentage of nasty customers who consistently behave badly all the time is rather small. That's not to say consistently nasty human beings don't exist. It's just that they are in the vast minority. Most unpleasant customers CAN behave pleasantly and respectfully given the right situations.

How about you? Have you ever lost your temper, yelled at someone, or made an obscene gesture? Maybe you have argued aggressively or pressured someone to get your way? Of course you have. These lapses into aggression are part of being human.

 Wise Thoughts To Ponder

Striking Out:
Have you ever "struck out" verbally at someone? Of course you have. Because of that you have it within you to understand angry customers and be a little bit more understanding.

Does it mean that you have some kind of personality defect or character problem as a human being? No. It means, that you ARE a human being. So are your customers.

That doesn't excuse aggressive or hostile behavior, though that's small consolation for the recipient of the aggression. What it does mean, though, is that your own angry behavior, just as with the angry behavior of your customers, is tied to the circumstances or situation you are in.

ANGER—THE FEELING

Anger refers to an internal state (it's a feeling) experienced by the person. An angry person experiences physiological changes, some invisible and some visible. Here are some important things about anger and angry people that will help you put customer anger in perspective.

Snapshot

Whose Anger?
All emotions belong to the person experiencing the emotion, and becoming angry (or not) is a choice you CAN make. This applies to you as well as your customer.

People **choose their emotional states**, although it doesn't always feel that way to them. Their feelings of anger, or for that matter, any feelings, **BELONG TO THEM**. As such the emotional state of your customers isn't your direct responsibility. That doesn't mean you ignore the feelings. Customer emotions affect you through the angry person's behavior. It's in your best interests to learn how to manage angry situations.

By recognizing that you can't directly control the emotions of another person, you are better able to step back from their anger, and not get caught up in it. What is your responsibility, however, is to ensure that you don't knowingly, or even unknowingly do things that are likely to provoke anger unnecessarily.

You need to accept the fact that customers will get angry. Customers have the right (just as you do), to have angry feelings. What customers don't have is the right to take the anger out in abusive, hostile or manipulative ways.

It's important that you become relatively comfortable with the notion that people will be angry. If you spend all your time trying to make your every customer happy, you are doomed to failure.

Wise Thoughts To Ponder

Everyone Happy?
It's impossible for us to satisfy and make happy each and every customer. You do your best, but sometimes the best outcome you can create is to minimize the impact of an unhappy customer. Agree?

ANGRY BEHAVIOR

Customers express anger in various ways. Some raise their voices or become more animated. Others turn red, and throw tantrums. Mild expressions of anger allow customers to vent a little steam. As with the feeling of anger, be reasonable in terms of what offends you, and allow the angry customer some latitude in behavior before you deem the behavior unacceptable.

There's a clear reason for this. If you allow yourself to be offended every time you encounter angry customer behavior, you will be pretty darned miserable, and pretty damned ineffective dealing with those difficult customer situations. As you'll see, the problems you must address have to do with hostile and abusive behavior, not angry behavior.

FROM THE ACCEPTABLE TO THE NON-ACCEPTABLE — HOSTILE AND ABUSIVE BEHAVIOR

There is a difference between reasonable expressions of anger (angry behavior) which is short lived and not aimed at you personally, and unacceptable behavior that we call hostile or abusive behavior. Not only are they different, but we may choose to handle these two different situations in different ways.

Hostile and abusive is intended, consciously or unconsciously, to have some or all of the following effects:

- Put you off balance
- Manipulate and control you
- Demean you in some way
- Cause you to feel guilty
- Cause you to experience other negative emotions
- Intimidate you

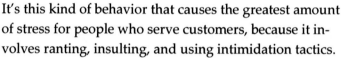

Snapshot

Thou Shalt Not Be Too Easily Offended:
Allow yourself to be offended every time you encounter angry customer behavior, and will be pretty darned miserable, and pretty darned ineffective dealing with those difficult customer situations.

It's this kind of behavior that causes the greatest amount of stress for people who serve customers, because it involves ranting, insulting, and using intimidation tactics.
Abusive behavior, because of the intent to elicit a reaction, involves pushing the buttons of customer service staff, making it more likely they will do something to makes the situation worse, not better.

While you may tolerate some degree of angry behavior without being concerned, hostile and abusive is something you do not want to accept. The primary goal, with abusive situations, is to cause the abusive behavior to stop. Once that occurs then you can work to reduce the angry feelings of the customer, and address his or her problem. You cannot help a person who is acting out or being abusive. It's virtually impossible. So, first stop the bad behavior (and we'll teach you how).

There are different "containers for abusive and hostile behavior, starting with verbal abuse.

 Bet You Didn't Know

Feelings & Behavior
The feeling of anger can only harm the person being angry through physiological changes. What we need to concern ourselves with in others is not their feelings of anger, but their angry behavior. The latter can hurt others.

VERBAL ABUSE

Verbal abuse takes many forms, from very subtle, to the more obvious, "in your face" behaviors. When we talk about verbal abuse we include the following:

- Persistent swearing
- Yelling
- Sexist comments (both explicit and implied)
- Racist comments (both explicit and implied)
- Irrelevant personal remarks (e.g. about your appearance)
- Threats (e.g. I'll have you fired)
- Intimidating silence
- Accusations of various sorts (e.g. calling you a racist)
- Comments about your competency, knowledge, dedication

These behaviors are intended to demean and control. As you go through this book, you will learn some ways to counter-control in the face of verbal abuse.

Non-Verbal Abuse

Non-verbal abuse includes manipulative behavior via body language, facial expressions, gestures, and physical outbursts like pounding on a counter. Unwanted physical touch/contact fits in this category.

Let's make no mistake about this. Non-verbal abuse is intended to send a message to you, such as *"I don't like you"*, or *"I'm fed up"*, or even *"In my eyes you are worth nothing"*. Non-verbal abuse is also often used as an intimidation tactic. Here are some examples:

- Standing in your personal space
- Starting at you (long eye contact)
- Table pounding
- Throwing things
- Leaning over you (using height advantage)
- Fearsome facial expressions
- Loud sighing
- Pointing, other offensive gestures

 CAUTION!

Listen Up Cowboy:
Unless you are a trained enforcement officer, do not ever confront someone physically, regardless of the size of the other person. No exceptions. Check your ego at the door.

Keep in mind that the customer showing these behaviors may not consciously intend them as intimidating or demeaning, but that doesn't lessen the effects or make them more acceptable.

As with verbal abuse, you want to take steps to stop those behaviors. Later on we will discuss specific counter-measures you can use to avoid being controlled by these non-verbal techniques.

THE EXTREME END — VIOLENCE

We can define violence as any action that is either intended to cause, or can cause physical harm to another person, be it you, a co-worker, or other customer. Some actions involving physical contact, such as arm grabbing or shoulder grabbing can be legally interpreted as assault, so we include them in this category, even if they cause no physical damage. Other actions, such as throwing things, would be considered violent behavior if there is intent to cause harm, or harm is done.

However, "acting-out" behavior such as ripping up papers and throwing them, or even sweeping things off a desk onto the floor are not "violent" within our definition. Abusive, yes. Hostile, yes. Scary? Indeed!

 Wise Thoughts To Ponder

Behavior of a Four Year Old:
Angry, frustrated adults often appear to act like spoiled four year olds. Why do you think that happens? Think about it. We'll explain it in the next chapter.

Generally this kind of violent behavior doesn't come out of the blue but is part of a sequence of events that involves verbal abuse. By learning to defuse hostility, and verbal abuse, you are more likely to reduce the potential for physical violence aimed at you. <u>Learning to defuse customers can make you safer at work.</u>

Your **first priority is to ensure your own physical safety, and the safety of those around you**. For this reason, most organizations accept that you have a right to remove yourself from a situation, or request backup assistance in situations where you feel physically threatened.

You don't have to be absolutely sure a physical threat exists. Don't take chances.

One final and critical point. Unless you are in a security or "enforcement" type job, and properly trained to deal with violence, you should never willingly engage in any physical altercation with a customer. Even in extreme situations, where you see someone shop-lifting, it's just plain dumb to pursue, confront, apprehend or get physically involved with the perpetrator, even if you have a significant size advantage. The reason is obvious. That slight, shoplifting teenager may be carrying a weapon in his pocket. It's not your job to run the risk, and you aren't trained for it.

 Snapshot

Focus on Behavior:
Throughout this book, we will focus on behavior, which is something we can influence. Our first priority is to assist the person in halting the abusive and destructive behavior. It is only once that is achieved that you do your job of helping solve a problem.

IMPLICATIONS FOR YOU

Let's summarize the implications for you— someone involved in customer service.

1.   While we all want people to like us, and not be angry with us, if we choose this as a goal, we are bound to be disappointed. Yes, it's good to try to meet the needs of our customers, so they are happier. Sometimes being liked just isn't in the cards.

2.   Anger is an emotion that belongs to the other person. You cannot be responsible for changing their emotions. It's not a realistic goal. Hostile and abusive behavior is another story. Focus your defusing efforts on reducing the amount and intensity of verbal and non-verbal hostile **behavior**. That is a realistic goal.

3.   In a later chapter, we'll examine the idea that abusive behavior is about control. The hostile customer tries to manipulate and control you, your emotions, and your decision-making. We want to make sure we don't allow this, or otherwise reinforce or "reward bad behavior". Later, we'll introduce specific ways to "counter-control".

4.   You need to provide some leeway for people to express their anger, provided the expressions are not demeaning, insulting, or manipulative. If you react to every four-letter word, customer twitch, or raised voice, you'll go nuts, and you won't be very good at defusing abusive customer situations. In other words, over-reaction, and over-sensitivity will end up increasing the amount of abuse you receive in these situations.

CHAPTER 3

WHERE DOES HOSTILE AND ABUSIVE BEHAVIOR COME FROM?

When we understand hostile behavior and how it works, we can better make sense of offensive and even counter productive behavior on the part of our customers. When we realize that much of this poor behavior is "normal" and not personal (even though it takes the form of personal attacks), we can remain in control of ourselves and the situation. Our understanding isn't used to excuse poor behavior or to give them more leeway. It's applied so we can shorten the aggression, communicate clear limits, and reduce the intensity of customer anger. Everyone wins.

 Wise Thoughts To Ponder

Adults and Children:
If you've noticed the similarity between adult angry behavior and child angry behavior, good for you. Both are build on the same foundation — a reinforcement cycle related to built in attention getting behavior that starts virtually at birth.

Besides this very practical point, it's quite interesting how people learn to be nasty. You will find that it is quite "normal" for people (and customers) to exhibit offensive behavior, and that human beings learn how to do this as part of the universal human development process. Let's reiterate that while everyone (even you) knows how to be nasty, that doesn't make it acceptable. Most people, having learned how to do it, also learn that it is not usually socially acceptable. Still, human beings are fallible.

THE CHILD

Think of infants as having a task – one that is hard wired into their brains. Infants need to master their environments, and how to act in it to receive the things they need to survive (food, contact, stimulation, etc.). They need to communicate with their caregivers (usually their parents) so they are taken care of. Of course, infants can't talk, so they can't say, "Golly, I sure am hungry".

Infants have other ways of communicating – more primitive ways they rely on to survive. They express their needs in ways parents can understand (well, at least sometimes), and react to. The infant is hungry. He might cry, move and kick, and turn red in the face. Or she might be wet and uncomfortable, and cry, move and kick, and turn red in the face. Truth to tell, crying, moving and kicking and turning red in the face are about the only things an infant CAN do to communicate.

What's the parent's natural response to the crying behavior? The parent tries to figure out the cause, and sets about fixing the situation. The infant's discomfort is removed, at least for the moment.

When you look at this cycle, you find a perfect example of what psychologists call "the effects of reinforcement". Most people call it the effects of reward. The infant behaves in an "angry" way. This signals the parent something needs to be done. The discomfort is removed, and the crying, or kicking and red face disappear at least for the moment. The removal of something uncomfortable reinforces the behavior preceding the removal (crying) as does receiving something pleasant (food, a cuddle).

Attending to a crying child is usually a good thing, but the infant learns that crying, moving and kicking, and turning red in the face are dandy ways of controlling the environment. When the child does these things, good things happen. We know that behaviors that are rewarded are repeated.

AS THE INFANT GETS OLDER

Bet You Didn't Know

Emotion and Behavior
When a person experiences intense emotion (usually called a high state of arousal), there is a strong tendency for the person to behave in more habitual, more primitive ways that are the "oldest" or most over-learned.

This simple principle explains a lot about human behaviour in stress situations.

Even before learning how to talk, the child refines his or her skills at controlling the environment with attention-getting behavior. Throwing a toy at the wall garners a response, although not always a positive one. As the infant moves into childhood, the range of behaviors expands, so with age becomes slightly more sophisticated behavior – sulking, pouting, making pleading noises and so on. The young child gets good at non-verbal "acting out" behavior.

Then language kicks in. As the child learns language, he or she acquires new tools to operate on the environment, to control it and manipulate it. Not surprisingly, since language overlays what is already learned (the non-verbal behaviors), early language is not always pleasant or "socialized". The child learns to say "NO", and how to ask for things in various tones of voice (begging, whining, use of angry tone and words). The child learns that certain words create commotion (e.g. swear words, and discovers that people can be influenced by them. The basics of verbal influence and manipulation emerge.

All of this is normal. The child learns to control the environment through angry and aggressive behavior. It's learned very early on. As people get older, they get better at it.

By the time the child becomes an adult, he or she has had a lot of practice, and developed expertise in influencing his or her environment, and earned how to:

- get people's attention
- make people mad
- invoke guilt feelings in others,
- influence the behaviors of others

It's a natural outgrowth of getting older. With age becomes additional sophistication. Think about teenagers. They have honed manipulative skills to a high degree and are in the process of establishing themselves as independent human beings. As they get older they will learn to better rein in manipulative behavior and control their own emotional states (so we hope, anyway). Meanwhile? Well, sometimes it gets rocky.

FINALLY, IN ADULTHOOD

The fact that children learn these behaviors doesn't mean they spend all their waking hours being abusive or manipulating others. As a counter-balance to wanton efforts to control the environment, children are also "socialized" (hopefully) so they learn that rampant controlling behavior is not always positively rewarding, and is often frowned upon by others. Again, in the teen years, adult "rules" have not yet sunk in, so teenagers tend to show more unfettered manipulation of others — i.e. Hostile behavior.

So here's a question. If most people learn that abusive, and aggressive behavior is not acceptable, how is it that we see so much of it?

One reason is that some people don't learn that this aggressive behavior is inappropriate. Another is that they've learned ways to justify bad behavior (rationalizations) to themselves. These are the people who are "rude and proud of it".

What about the others? What about people who know that aggressive behavior is not acceptable? A lot of "regular" people, use aggressive and manipulative techniques. Perhaps every one of us does, at least sometimes. A little more knowledge about human behavior can help us understand why people use hostile behavior.

Learning is a funny thing. It isn't a question of whether something is learned or not, but rather how well something is learned, that dictates whether it is used. In other words some things are not learned well, others are learned pretty well, and some things are learned very well, to the point where the person doesn't even have to think about carrying out the learned tasks. Some examples of the latter include driving, tying shoelaces, walking, and in fact many every day things we do without having to think about them.

We call these latter actions, <u>over learned </u>actions – things that are learned really well, and practiced so often and so well that the person is unlikely to forget.

We also know that under normal circumstances a person who has learned something "pretty well", will use what they have learned when and if it is appropriate and its use seems rational to the person. The person thinks, decides, then acts. This chain of events happens quickly, but there's a decidedly rational or "thought out" component.

The exception occurs when the person is emotionally upset. When people are upset they revert back to earlier, more primitive and **<u>better learned behavior.</u>**

Consider a regular person who has learned a number of communication skills effective in conflict and problem solving situations. Normally, when faced with situations where he/she is not overly upset, the person uses these constructive skills. The problem comes when the person is very angry, Adrenaline pumps. Emotions have started the climb into overdrive.

If the person becomes sufficiently "activated", he or she will revert back to behavior learned earlier in life (and therefore well practiced and over learned). What behaviors? You guessed it. The more primitive, angry and aggressive behaviors that worked in early life, re-emerge in the normally rational, calm adult. That's what happens with your hostile customers.

As a test of this, have you ever noticed that adults who are hostile and aggressive often behave like small children? They are reverting to older, over learned behavior.

Some hostile customers are habitually nasty. Most, though, are normally rather polite people who have let their emotions run away from them. Out comes the more childish behaviors they have over learned during their lives.

Consider also that most hostile customers, although they may appear to be trying to consciously manipulate you, are not plotting and scheming to get you.

It doesn't work that way. Reversion just happens and it usually does not involve conscious intent. Very few individuals actually plot out aggressive strategies in a conscious manner. In a sense most people are just acting human when they become more aggressive. They are doing what they are able to do, and what they are "good at". Given their emotional states, they automatically go back to what they know how to do well (i.e. that which was learned long ago, and well practiced).

This does not excuse abusive behavior. **The point here is that those people react to their internal states, not to you personally.**

Turning Theory Into Practice

Now that we have explained where and when hostile behavior is learned, we can see that its major purpose is to control or manipulate the environment. Applied to your hostile customers, it's a logical extension to say "One of the major purposes of customer aggression involves controlling you and trying to influence your reactions in the almost naïve hope that you will do whatever it is the customer wants." It really doesn't have to make sense in a logical and rational way, but since these tactics are embedded in childhood experience, they don't HAVE to make rational sense.

Understanding this helps us discover some critical principles regarding defusing these hostile situations. You will apply this understanding throughout the book as we help you translate knowledge into practical defusing strategies and tactics. For the moment, we need to examine the importance of not allowing ourselves to be controlled by this behavior. That means we must avoid responding to nasty attacks in ways that the attacker wants. We want to remove the rewards for bad behavior from the equation.

If you refuse to be controlled, and refuse to react the way your attacker wishes, they you will be a good way towards stopping the attack.

The Rules of The Abuse/Attack Game

If you deal with irate customers regularly, you've probably noticed that the attacks and aggressive tactics they use are quite similar. A common comment by veterans in the customer contact areas is that they "have heard it all before". They rarely hear anything new.

You're already familiar with the body language, tone of voice, specific words, and specific attacks used, since they tend to repeat. Within any one culture, there is only a finite number of ways people can be hostile.

Hostile behavior follows rules, just like a game. The behavior that occurs in hostile situations is characterized by certain patterns that repeat over and over again. If you consider hostile interactions within the framework of a game, albeit a serious one, and understand that it's played according to a set of rules, learning those rules will help you understand what to do when dealing with aggressive customer behavior.

 Snapshot

Unlike most games, where it is a good thing to follow the rules, when it comes to dealing with and defusing hostile behaviour, following the rules is a bad thing. The rules of the abuse game are primitive and child based, and following them tends to escalate conflict and verbal attacks.

Imagine a game — chess, or checkers, or Monopoly where one person defies or ignores the rules of play. At that point, the game MUST end. The game of abuse/attack works just like that, only it's a game that you want to end, not one you want to continue playing.

Before we discuss the two major rules of hostile interactions, we need to introduce the concept of "bait".

Bait — Hook, Line and Sinker

Earlier we said that the major purpose or goal of the attacker is to control your emotional reactions and behavior. The attacker wants to take and hold the initiative, and force you to react and respond to him, rather than the other way around. As long as the attacker can maintain this conversational control, the unpleasant interaction will continue. This isn't good because while you focus on reacting and responding, you won't be able to help the customer, or find a way to end the interaction in a positive way.

The primary way the attacker uses to maintain control involves "bait". Bait consists of behaviors (verbal and non-verbal) designed to get you to react, usually in an emotional way. If you respond to the bait, you hand over control of the conversation to the attacker, which is exactly what he/she wants. The bait is used to upset you enough so you will be off balance emotionally.

Take a look at the dialogue below:

> **Customer:** "What the hell is wrong with you. Every time I come here to try to resolve this, you hassle me and give me the runaround. If you had a clue about your job, this wouldn't happen. And this is the last time you are going to do this to me".
>
> **Employee:** "How dare you talk to me like that. I do my best to help and you don't even see that we're short-staffed…"
>
> **Customer:** "I can talk to you any way I want. I pay your salary! You work for me!

Look carefully at the customer's first statements. Has the person said anything that is **NOT** blaming, demeaning, threatening, or otherwise emotionally provocative? No. It's ALL bait. The ONLY message embedded in that mess of insulting words is "I'm angry". That's it. The words are bait.

Snapshot

When you "take the bait" (respond to the irrelevant details of the verbal attack), you will increase the time and intensity of the verbal attacks. You don't deal with bait directly. There are other indirect and constructive ways.

Look at how the employee responds. He "takes the bait", and loses any control over the direction of the conversation. He responds aggressively ("How dare you talk to me like that"), and then defensively. The most important thing here is that the employee takes the bait, responds to the attacking remarks and ends up being controlled.

In turn, the customer replies with additional bait. This is not heading in a constructive direction, particularly if the employee allows himself to be lead by the nose into acting badly himself.

This is typical of situations where an employee takes the bait. The employee's reaction sends a few "sub-messages" to the customer. First, the customer knows he has found gaps in the employee's armor, and knows (largely unconsciously) that he can maintain control if he continues to bait and act aggressively and in an insulting way.

Second, the customer knows he can upset the employee. The upshot is that the attacks will probably continue, since the customer is getting what he wants psychologically – control over the employee and the interactions. He's being rewarded for bad behavior.

Let's take a look at the dialogue shown on the next page, where the employee does NOT reward the bad behavior.

Notice the difference? The employee doesn't take the bait dangled by the customer, and works to reassert control over the interaction. He does this by acknowledging the person's anger, and NOT

> **Customer:** "What the hell is wrong with you. Every time I come here to try to resolve this, you hassle me and give me the runaround. If you had a clue about your job, this wouldn't happen. And this is the last time you are going to do this to me".
>
> **Employee:** "Mr. Smith, you really sound upset about this."
>
> **Customer:** "Damn right I'm upset. What are you going to do about this?"
>
> **Employee:** I need some information from you so I can help. Can you give me your file number?"
>
> **Customer:** "It's B05949".

exploring any of the baiting remarks. At the end of this short dialogue, the customer begins to respond to the employee, and work with him. This conversation is much more likely to be shorter, more productive, and less upsetting than the one where the employee swallows the bait.

The key point is that the attacker expects you to take the bait. It's in the rules of the hostility game.

The psychological rule used by the customer goes like this:

"If I use bait, the other person will react to it in ways that will allow me to maintain control".

So, you want to break this rule of the game. After all, why should you play a game defined by the attacker, which you will lose? You need to set up a new game, with a different set of rules, and the first step is not to play by the attacker's rules, on the attacker's turf.

Don't take bait. Recognize it for what it is, an attempt by the other person to control and irritate you. Later on we'll talk about specific responses you can make that take you out of the hostile game. For now, remember that bait hides a nasty barbed hook. Stay away from it.

 Wise Thoughts To Ponder

How we deal with intention:
When we believe someone is intentionally trying to harm us, we tend to react with more anger and fury than if we believe the person is harming us accidentally. That is why it is important to understand that much verbal aggression is not planned.

MORE RULES

There are a few more rules about hostile interactions that are important to understand, since knowing those "rules" will help you avoid getting drawn into the "attack game".

When you are attacked, the rules specify that **you will respond in a knee jerk, almost automatic way**, with one of two expected responses. YOUR responses, just like those of the attacker, are learned very young, which is why they tend to be automatic — executed without reflection or thinking. Unfortunately, these "child" responses to attacks almost guarantee that the attack will continue and escalate.

Do Not Follow Rule 1: When Attacked You Will Respond Defensively.

This rule specifies that when attacked, you will attempt to defend yourself (or your company). Often this defense consists of denying the charge leveled at you. Here are some examples:

- I only work here
- I try the best I can
- We're short-staffed
- I am treating you fairly
- I know what I'm doing
- We don't lose files

Defensive statements almost always have the word "I" in them, or the word "we".

Do Not Follow Rule 2: When Attacked You Will Counter-Attack.

This rule specifies that when attacked, you will counter-attack., A counter-attack is an attempt to use abusive and manipulative techniques aimed at the initial attacker — insults, sarcasm, intimidation and so on. Counter-attacks are conveyed through the actual words, or the tone of voice and non-verbals. Common counter-attacking remarks include:

- You have no right to talk to me like that
- You don't know what you are talking about
- Get out
- It's too bad your parents didn't teach you manners

Counter-attacks almost always contain the word "YOU" in them, although sometimes the "you" is implied (e.g. Get out!).

The two rules above define what the attacker <u>EXPECTS</u> from you according to the game the attacker is playing. If you play by the attacker's rules, ultimately you lose. You lose time, and you encourage the attack to continue. Although defending and counter-attacking are "natural" responses to attacks, they almost always make things worse.

So, to summarize this section:

1. Stop responding to bait. The attacker wants you to take the bait, and when you do, you are trapped inside the abuse/attack game.

2. Avoid responding with defensive statements, no matter how tempting. If you use a defensive statement, you play the attacker's game by the attacker's rules, and you end up manipulated and controlled.

3. Avoid counter-attacking for the same reasons stated above.

Remember that when you do what the attacker expects, the attacker will continue to attack without skipping a beat. The key, as you will see later, is to respond to attacks in unexpected ways. That forces the attacker to stop using old, childish forms of interaction, since they no longer receive the expected or usual responses from you.

What Angry People Need And Want

When dealing with an angry customer, have you ever asked yourself "What the heck does this person want from me?".

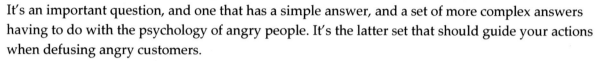

It's an important question, and one that has a simple answer, and a set of more complex answers having to do with the psychology of angry people. It's the latter set that should guide your actions when defusing angry customers.

They Want What They Want

This is the simple answer. The angry customer appears to want his or her problem or complaint fixed. Sometimes what the customer "wants" is completely unreasonable, or impossible to provide. In other situations, you can fix some or all of what the customer wants. What's interesting here is that even when you resolve the customer's problem, the customer does not necessarily let go of his or her anger. Why? Because customer anger comes from two sources. The first is not getting what he wants when he wants it, but the second source has to do with how he or she is treated and whether his or her psychological needs are addressed. Fulfill these psychological needs and wants and you will reduce hostile behavior, even if you can't do what the customer wants you to do.

They Want Help/Effort On Their Behalf

Angry or hostile people want you to be helpful, even if you can't solve their entire problem. If the customer sees you are making a genuine effort, he or she is much less likely to be hostile towards you personally.

Think about your own experiences as a customer. Have you ever gone into a department store to make a purchase and had difficulty finding the item you wanted? After searching for what seems like an eternity, you finally find a staff person. You ask the employee where you might find the item, and you get the following response:

"Don't know. That's not my department."

Infuriating, isn't it? But why? You aren't any worse off than before. You are no farther from the product you want. The reason is simply psychological. The disinterested employee is saying to you

"You don't mean squat to me, not even enough to bother trying on your behalf". That's not what the actual words say but that's the meaning embedded underneath the words.

No matter how secure you are in yourself, being treated as if you are unimportant, irrelevant, or an annoyance is perceived as an attack on the self. Now you have two reasons to be angry. First there's the frustration of not being able to find the product. Second is being treated badly. The second one becomes the more important and is what will drive your actions.

What if the employee responded as follows:

"Golly, I don't know, but if you wait a moment I can find out."

That would be an entirely different story. When you make an effort to help a customer, or at least try to help, your customers are less likely to strike out at you.

By making the effort, you show the customer that you consider the person as IMPORTANT. When you "blow off" a customer, you show the customer that you think the customer is UNIMPORTANT. A lack of effort is psychologically demeaning to the customer, which is why he or she escalates the intensity of the anger.

 CAUTION!

Avoid:
Here's an example of a phrase that sends the message that the customer is not unique or special: "**Nobody else has complained about the service.**" Can you see how this provokes an argument and extends an aggressive interaction?

CUSTOMERS WANT CHOICES

Nobody likes to feel helpless, trapped or without choices. When people (and by extension, customers) feel helpless, or feel there is nothing they can do, they experience frustration, and that results in angry behavior. It's important that you offer choices and options to customers. You'll find offering choices, no matter how small, goes a long way to making the customer feel both valued and empowered.

Here's an example. You answer the phone and the caller asks to speak to Jessica Jones. Ms. Jones is out of the office at the moment. You say:

"I'm sorry but Ms Jones is away from her desk at the moment. I will take a message and she will call you back."

That's not a bad response, at least on the surface. What it lacks is an offer of choice made to the caller. Here's an alternative that incorporates choice.

"I'm sorry but Ms. Jones is away from her desk. Would you like her to call you back at a particular time, or would you prefer to call again after 3:00, when she will be available?"

That's much better, but the difference is subtle. The first response offers no options, but the second allows the caller to choose, or to suggest some other possibility that might be workable. The second example is much less likely to "set off" the customer.

There are always choices to offer. We know that customers respond positively to being offered choices, since it reduces their own sense of helplessness.

CUSTOMERS WANT ACKNOWLEDGEMENT AS INDIVIDUALS

One of the most important things an angry person wants is to be acknowledged and understood as a unique individual. Customers want to feel that you are trying to understand both their situation, AND their emotional reactions to it, and that you are not treating them as if they are like every other customer.

Each person feels their situation is somehow unique and special. While that is probably rarely the case, woe betide the customer service representative that tries to make the customer feel like "just another customer". This isn't just about being nice, by the way. If you contradict, accidentally or on purpose, the person's perception of specialness, the person will lash out.

Often the simple act of acknowledging that a person is upset will help to calm the person down, provided the acknowledgement is phrased and toned correctly.

The most common error customer service staff makes when dealing with angry clients is to ignore the feelings being expressed and shift immediately into a problem-solving mode. While that's well intentioned and seems to be "common sense", it's often the wrong thing to do. Customers perceive a move to problem solving without acknowledgement as uncaring, unfeeling and unhelpful. That sets you up for further aggression.

It's critically important to acknowledge the customer's emotions. Later, when we talk about specific techniques and phrases, we'll explain how to use empathy and active listening statements and questions to prove to the customer that you care, and that you understand "where they are coming from".

CUSTOMERS WANT A SENSE OF EQUALITY AND FAIRNESS

Now it gets a little strange. While customers want to feel special and acknowledged as individuals, they also want to feel they are being treated like everyone else. It's a bit of a paradox since, on one hand the customer feels she is special, but on the other she doesn't want to receive LESS than other customers. Never mind what's real, though, because it is the perception of the customer that determines their approach to you.

The point here is that you will need to convey that you are treating the person as an individual with individual needs and wants while at the same time also conveying that they are not receiving LESS than someone else might in the situation. Well, nobody said humans are perfect.

The Escalation/Crisis Cycle

Initial Contact

Customer is ready to get angry
reactive
sensitive
feels powerless
feels depersonalized
fearful
feels unimportant

Employee Response / Action

Bureaucratic response
Gets triggered, takes bait
Responds defensively
Coldness or terseness
Unhelpful or passive
Lack of listening and impatience

Customer Reactions

Increased frustration
Higher sense of helplessness
and fear
Increases aggression
Becomes more abusive

Employee Reaction

Defends or counter-attacks
more triggered
less self-control
more aggressive or colder
even less helpful sounding

Escalation
to
CRISIS

Loss of
Control

Violence
Potential

SECTION SUMMARY

To summarize, angry customers want you to fix their problem but often this isn't possible, and it's not "enough" to fix the problem. They also want:

- Helpfulness and effort on your part
- To feel they have options and choices and are not helpless
- Acknowledgement of their situation and their feelings, and their individuality
- Fairness and equality

By recognizing these "wants" and providing for them, you can have a significant impact on the hostility directed at you. If you ignore them you will spend a lot of unnecessary time in arguments and being the target of hostile behavior.

UNDERSTANDING THE ESCALATION CYCLE

Angry situations don't always start with very abusive or hostile behavior. Even a benign conversation can become acrimonious and destructive if each person's behavior "triggers" aggressive behavior in the other. This process — the escalation cycle is, no doubt familiar to you because it often happens in close family relationships. If you have two family members who know each other well enough to "push each others' buttons", you have a situation where the escalation cycle is likely to occur.

Even a conversation that starts out playfully or pleasantly can escalate this way. Escalation is even more likely to happen when one or both people are angry in the first place, or one or both people are stressed and tired.

The escalation cycle is a process where an individual becomes hostile or enters in an angry state of mind. If the customer is not treated in a way that helps him or her feel important and listened to, the customer gets more and more frustrated and abusive. In a typical escalation cycle, the employee over-reacts, which in turn, increases the anger of the client. If the cycle is not interrupted, the situation becomes an out-of-control crisis situation. That's when people can get hurt.

Escalation doesn't have to happen. It is important that you be aware of your own behavior in contributing to this cycle, particularly because you will bear the stress problems that a crisis bring. When the situation moves to crisis, the probability of violence increases, as does the probability that the person will cause unpleasantness after leaving by going to the media, complaining to a senior company official, calling a talk show or posting nasty messages on the Internet.

 Snapshot

1) Stop responding to bait.
2) Avoid responding with defensive statements ((Try not to use I or We as the subject).
3) Avoid counter-attacking.

In many cases the cycle can be stopped by stepping back from the situation, not taking the bait, and appearing helpful, offering choices and acknowledging

EARLY in the interaction. The escalation cycle needs to be stopped as early as possible, before it develops its own head of steam. It's a lot easier to prevent hostile behavior than to deal with it once it's full blown.

The escalation/crisis cycle is diagrammed on page 28. Many of the tactics in this book are used to stop the cycle early on, and quickly. By doing so, you save both time and stress, since you reduce both the length and intensity of angry interactions with customers.

Chapter IV

The Defusing Process & The C.A.R.P. System

W e introduce The CARP System, a master strategy for defusing hostility, and discuss a number of important defusing principles you can use to guide your actions.

OVERVIEW OF THE DEFUSING PROCESS

In the last chapter we discussed the nature of anger, hostile behavior, and abusive behavior. In this chapter you will learn some basic principles regarding **defusing hostility**. As we move forward you will see very specific techniques and specific language to use, along with other defusing techniques.

Before we do that, let's do a little review of the key points in the last chapter.

- ♦ At times your clients are going to be angry, and you need to recognize they have a right to be upset or angry.

- ♦ Your clients do NOT have the right to be abusive, or manipulative.

- ♦ You need to focus your attention on ways that will reduce the amount of hostile behavior aimed at you. If these techniques cause the customer to feel less angry, that's great. But that isn't something we can control.

Snapshot
You need to focus your attention on ways that will reduce the amount of hostile behaviour aimed at you. If these techniques cause the customer to feel less angry, that's great. But that isn't something we can control.

- ♦ Hostile and abusive behavior is intended to control and manipulate you.

- ♦ Hostile and abusive behavior is learned at a very young age, and everyone has learned how to do it.

- ♦ Hostile people will dangle bait in front of you. The first step in avoiding escalation of these situations is to not take the bait.

- ♦ The rules of the hostile "game" say that when attacked, you **are EXPECTED** to respond defensively, or by counter-attacking. When you do so you play the game according to the attacker's rules, and you will lose.

- ♦ While angry people want their problem solved, they will also respond positively if you:

  - • Appear helpful

- Offer choices
- Acknowledge their feelings and individuality
- Help develop the perception of fairness and equality

♦ Hostile situations can escalate very quickly. One key to defusing is to control the interaction from square one, and avoid doing things that will cause the escalation cycle to continue.

The CARP System — A Master Strategy

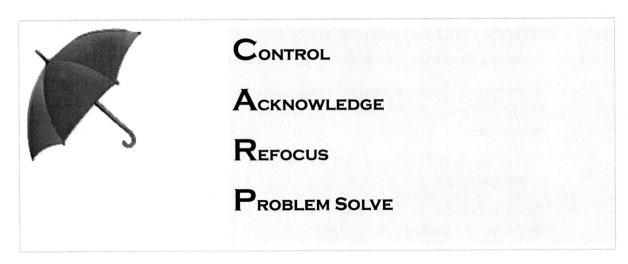

CONTROL

ACKNOWLEDGE

REFOCUS

PROBLEM **S**OLVE

The CARP System is a way to remind yourself of the four major pieces of the defusing hostility process. It's what we call an umbrella strategy because it shelters us from abuse, and guides our actions.

The CARP process consists of four somewhat sequential parts.

Let's go through these one by one.

CONTROL

Snapshot

Key To Conversational Control: The key in reasserting control is to behave in ways that send the subtle sub-message **"your techniques will not work on me".**

When you communicate with an irate customer, they will often "take the floor", refusing to listen to you. Often, they will take a verbally attacking position, pepper you with questions or insults, and not let you get a word in edgewise. This is particularly pronounced on the phone, but also occurs in person. Some have characterized the behavior of the irate person as "ranting".

In addition to the verbal behavior of the irate customer, they may use nonverbal behavior to intimidate, anger, or otherwise make you feel uncomfortable. They may move into your space, stare, and glare, and attempt to use height to their advantage.

As we have said before, the customer attempts to control the interaction, by causing you to become defensive, angry or off balance.

<u>Your first goal in the defusing process is to gain control over the interaction.</u> You need to get the person to the point where they are willing to stop talking and listen. If they don't stop their "rant", then there is not much chance of a positive outcome. Also, you may need to control the interaction non-verbally, so that the person stops using nonverbal intimidation tactics to put you off balance.

As you will see when we talk about specific ways of controlling the interaction, we want to be as subtle as possible in reasserting control. Telling a customer to *"get out of my face"* is not likely to work very well.

The key in reasserting control is to behave in ways that send the subtle sub message "<u>Your techniques are not going to work on me</u>".

While we will get into specific techniques later, now would be a good time to provide you with an example of how one employee was able to re-assert control of a hostile interaction.

Picture a successful financial services company. The organization deals directly with the public, and has several storefront operations. It's like a bank where people line up and are served at a window when their turn comes.

Mr. Jones walks in, and after waiting in line, arrives at the wicket. He asks for what he wants and the employee, Fred, informs the client that he must fill in a series of forms, and provide some documents (i.e.. birth certificate, etc.). Mr. Jones starts getting angrier and angrier, and says:

> *"Why the hell didn't anyone tell me about this before. You want me to spend the next hour filling out your damn forms, and on top of that you need a birth certificate ... why the heck can't I just use my driver's license. You guys are so stupid and inefficient .. I am sick of having my tax money support your inefficiency. "*
>
> **Fred replies:** *"Sir, I know it's frustrating, but we can't process your application without the forms being filled out and the birth certificate. Why don't you just fill out the forms?"*

This doesn't help at all, and the customer continues on.

"Because I have better things to do with my time, it's too bad you don't. You know what you can do with your F***** forms? You can take them and shove 'em where the sun don't shine". [Actually he used more graphic language].

Fred replies: "Mr. Jones, I would love to oblige you on that, but unfortunately, I have five file folders, six other forms and a large filing cabinet up there, and quite honestly, I don't think that there is room for much more ".

Mr. Jones stops talking for a moment. When he realizes what the employee has said, his jaw drops. Then after a second or two, he starts laughing. Fred joins in.

Mr. Jones says: *"Look, I'm sorry. I'm having a bad day, and I don't mean to take it out on you. Do I really have to do all this?"*

Fred replies: *"I know you are frustrated, but yes, we need the forms done. Can I make a suggestion as to how you might do this as quickly as possible, so you don't spend anymore time than necessary"*

Mr. Jones replies: *"Yeah, OK"*

QUICK ANALYSIS:

Notice what happened here. Fred, took advantage of an unusual, unexpected remark (humor) to stun the customer into giving up the floor. He used humor to surprise and defuse the customer's anger. It probably hasn't escaped your notice that this could have backfired very badly. We'll get back to that a bit later in the chapter.

The important thing to note is that Fred gained control of the interaction so that he could move on to a more productive discussion.

ACKNOWLEDGE

The **A** in CARP stands for acknowledge. Remember it is important that the angry customer see that you understand his/her emotional state, and the situation. So, when we talk about acknowledging, we are talking about two major techniques, empathy and active listening.

Snapshot

More on CARP Sequences
The CARP model gives you a rough idea of the sequence of defusing steps but the process must be flexible. Sometimes you need to go back and forth between the steps, and sometimes you actually do several things at once. The one thing to remember is that you must control the interaction and calm the person before problem-solving.

The key point here is that a person's anger will tend to diminish if the person feels you understand them. Again, we will talk about ways that work and ways that don't when we get to specific techniques.

Refocus

The **R** in CARP refers to refocus. When a customer comes in and is angry, or becomes angry, that anger interferes with your ability to work with the customer quickly and effectively. The control and acknowledge components are designed to calm the person down somewhat. Refocusing involves making the transition from dealing with emotions to dealing with the actual problem.

Note the sequence. We do not attempt to deal with the problem until we have dealt with the feelings first. This is VERY important.

Problem Solve

The **P** in CARP stands for problem solving.

Before we move to problem solving, we look to see that the person has become more cooperative, less emotional, and more rational. Refocusing provides the transition to "getting down to business". Problem solving involves actions like getting and giving information, suggesting possibilities and appearing helpful, offering choices as available, agreeing on a course of action, and following through.

Snapshot

Sequence:
The sequence of the CARP system is very important. While you may try to gain control and acknowledge almost at the same time, it's really important that you don't jump to problem solving too early.

Points To Remember

The sequence of the CARP system is important. While you may try to gain control and acknowledge almost at the same time, what is really important is that you don't jump to problem solving too early. How do you know if it is too early?

When you find yourself explaining the same thing over and over, or the customer is just not listening and continues to interrupt, these are hints that the customer isn't ready to deal with the problem. If this occurs, go back to the acknowledgment component.

Remember that **ALL** four components are necessary to effective defusing. To illustrate, another story is in order.

I had the opportunity to deliver a defusing hostility seminar to a group of people. In that group was a manager, who we will call Roger. Roger liked the course, and said he found the course very valuable.

About a year later, Roger called me up, and said he wanted me to deliver the seminar to his staff. I agreed and we set up a few seminars.

At one of those seminars, I talked about the importance of acknowledgment, and was talking about using empathy. Several of the staff there found this quite amusing, and were whispering to one another. I was curious as to what was happening (I always like a good joke), and at break time, asked the two people what they found amusing. One of the fellows responded: *"Well, now we know where Roger got that empathy stuff."*

His tone indicated that this was not a completely positive statement, so I asked what he meant. He replied: *"Well, let me put it this way. I go into Roger's office to complain about the antiquated computer equipment. After explaining how bad it is, and that we need to do something about it, Roger usually says something like 'You seem really frustrated about this'. Then I explain that I am frustrated, and we must do something about the equipment. Roger will say something like 'It must be very frustrating'. After a few minutes, I usually give up."*

Now, the problem with Roger is he glommed on to the acknowledgment part, but hadn't figured out he had to refocus and problem solve, or he would come off as an idiot. He didn't use all of the CARP components. He appeared less than genuine. It was clear to staff that ole Roger wasn't going to DO anything to actually help. Acknowledgement and empathy are great tools, but being useful is important too.

If you think about it, it is rather amazing than the staff didn't throttle Roger.

PRINCIPLES OF DEFUSING

Let's look at a set of principles that you can use to guide your defusing efforts. In the next chapter we will move to much more specific actions and phrases.

PRINCIPLE 1: DEAL WITH THE FEELINGS FIRST

A fundamental principle of defusing is that you must deal with the anger and frustration first, since an angry person tends to think unclearly, and less rationally. The primary technique to deal with the feelings is empathy, a way of acknowledging the person's upset.

PRINCIPLE 2: AVOID COMING ACROSS AS BUREAUCRATIC

 Snapshot

One person may respond very well to a most gentle approach. Another person may respond to a firm tone, while someone else may require you to be almost aggressive. You must use your judgment and experience, since you are the one interacting with the person.

Traditionally, large corporations (e.g.. banks, chain stores, telecommunications) and their employees have been viewed as unfeeling, uncaring, rigid and overly formal and officious. Some of these employees seem to believe that if they are aloof, very formal, and talk in complicated language, they will gain more respect from clients. Unfortunately, the exact opposite is the case. The more bureaucratic you sound, the more likely you are to infuriate the customer.

There are several reasons for this. In Psychology there is a term called objectification, which refers to the process where a person is seen as an object or thing. The notion of objectification has been cited as one contributor to abuse of women.

What we know is that the more a person sees you as a gear in the bureaucratic machinery, the more he/she can see you as an object. And this means, more abuse. However, if you come across as a real human being, with a name, and feelings, the hostile individual is less likely to aim anger and hostile behavior at you.

A second reason to consider relates to the source of the person's anger. Although they may express their frustration in ways that seem very personal to you, in the form of slurs, and other attacks, their anger is primarily about the system that they are interacting with. You are just a handy target. The more they see you as "that system" the more they are likely to address their frustration at you.

 Wise Thoughts To Ponder

Momentum
Emotions develop momentum, at least until fatigue sets in. The longer the customer is angry, the worse the anger tends to get and the harder it is to defuse it. Hence, you start defusing from the first contact.

When dealing with clients, avoid coming across as bureaucratic. It's better to express a bit of personality, smile, and use the person's name, and your name if possible. Also avoid bureaucratic language. For example, rather than reading from a policy or corporate document, explain it in common language, while making the original text available. Stay away from harsh language that can be interpreted as inflexible (see section on cooperative language). And stay away from the expression "It's against policy", or anything similar. If you need to explain a policy, introduce your explanation with something like:

"Let me explain how we usually do things. We ask that you... "

In other words, talk like a live human being, not a bureaucrat. You can say whatever you need to say in a helpful, cooperative and human way. You don't need to be the bureaucrat.

By the way, many members of the public may expect you to be cold, distant, and formal because of the nature of your service. They have very low expectations of you even before you have met. By not fitting these expectations, you throw the angry person off, making it more difficult for you to be targeted for abuse. A good example of turning a negative (expectations) into a positive.

 CAUTION!

Three Part Assertive Statements Fail
Avoid using three part assertive statements with angry customers who don't know you and don't care about you. They have little interest in your feelings.

PRINCIPLE 3: EACH PERSON/SITUATION IS DIFFERENT

Each person you deal with is slightly different. One person may respond very well to a gentle approach. Another person may respond to a firm tone, while someone else may require you to be almost aggressive. You must use your judgment and experience, since you are the one interacting with the person.

What this means is that you must observe the person carefully, watching to see if anything in particular is working. If you try several empathy responses and the person gets more hostile, either you are mis-phrasing your responses (tone, words), or, empathy just isn't going to work with that person. You decide. You try out techniques, and look to see what happens. If it works, keep doing it and if it doesn't, try something different. Keep in mind that memorized scripts are always a bad idea. Apart from the fact that each situation is different, and requires a slightly different (flexible) approach that scripts cannot provide, customers can tell whether you are reciting something memorized or interacting with them in real time dialogue. People overwhelmingly prefer conversations with people who converse like people, and dislike scripted interactions.

PRINCIPLE 4: STRIVE TO CONTROL THE INTERACTION

When dealing with a hostile person your two primary tasks are to acknowledge their feelings and get them to start responding to you. Often, you will be doing both at the same time. Remember that if you can't get control, you can't accomplish anything.

PRINCIPLE 5: BEGIN DEFUSING EARLY

In an earlier section we discussed the escalation cycle, and how angry interactions tend to escalate with time, unless one person gets off the merry-go-round. The more the situation escalates, the more time, energy and upset it is going to create. Begin defusing early. In fact, you can pre-empt angry attacks by taking control of the interaction immediately (be the first person to speak), and empathize, even before the angry person has had a chance to launch the first salvo. One thing that will help you defuse early is to look for nonverbal indications that your client is upset, as they approach you. If they look tense, glance at their watch, scowl, etc., be sure to defuse immediately.

PRINCIPLE 6: BE ASSERTIVE, NOT AGGRESSIVE OR PASSIVE

Being assertive means that you act in a confident way, and that you talk calmly but firmly, if necessary. It also means that your physical posture must be confident rather than too passive or aggressive.

If you have taken an assertiveness training course, you will doubtless be familiar with assertive language such as:

> " When you yell at me, I feel upset. I would like you to stop yelling, or I am going to end our conversation. "   or

"When you get too close to me, I feel trapped. I would like you to step back, or I am going to ask you to leave."

We **DO NOT** suggest you use this type of language with angry clients. It is fine with people with whom you have relationships, but remember that the angry client isn't particularly interested in your feelings. They are concerned about their own feelings, and want to hear you recognize them rather than vice versa.

Bet You Didn't Know

The Attention Paradox
Remember this: What you pay attention to, or focus upon, you get more of. Focus on how idiotic the customer is, and you'll probably get more of the same. Focus on his negative comments, and again, you'll get more.

Leave out references to your own emotions, unless you are interacting with a customer you might have known for a long time. If the person is someone you believe does care about your feelings, then it makes sense to mention them. Remember most customers, at least when angry, simply don't care if you are offended.

Being assertive means being firm, sounding and looking confident, and recognizing that, you too, have rights.

Now, let's look at aggressiveness and passivity. Most of us know how to be aggressive. The aggressive person uses very harsh language, a tone of voice that sounds angry, and projects a physically confrontational stance. Note that we include any expressions of frustration in this category of behavior, such as sighing, rolling the eyes, etc. That's aggressive too.

The problem with aggressive behavior is that it invites confrontation and argument. If you want to spend half an hour arguing over some off topic point, or if you want to put yourself at risk physically, then be aggressive. If, however, you want to deal with the client professionally and quickly, and increase your own safety, then be firm, assertive and calm.

At the other end of the spectrum is passivity. Passive people tend not to stand up for themselves, use a tone of voice that is whiny or weak sounding, and tend to use a body posture that looks powerless. Some people believe that the more passive you are the less likely people are to be nasty to you. The problem with this is that passivity will entice a bully to redouble their efforts at intimidation. They will sense your discomfort, and continue to attack if they feel you are off balance or weak.

Again, assertiveness is the key. Firm but cooperative language and tone is the best choice and avoids creating confrontations, or appearing like you have a "kick me" sign on your butt.

PRINCIPLE 7: IF YOU LOSE CONTROL OF YOUR EMOTIONS, YOU LOSE. PERIOD

Perhaps the very worst thing you can do with a hostile person is to lose control over your own emotions. When you allow yourself to get angry and respond aggressively, you are going to have an argument or a physical confrontation. If you get angry and make a snarky remark, or use hostile body language, you will simply provoke the person to continue.

What we stress here is that while you are allowed to be angry or upset with a customer, you are not allowed to "take it out" on that customer. It isn't so much an issue of what's right or what's wrong ... it's a very practical issue. Allow yourself to get your buttons pushed, and you are letting yourself in for a string of hassles that you don't need.

CAUTION!

The problem with aggressive behavior is that it invites confrontation and argument. If you want to spend half an hour arguing over some off-topic point, or if you want to put yourself at risk physically, then be aggressive.

Normally, when we talk about self-control, we talk about anger control, but there is another issue. Hostile people don't just do things that contribute to your anger. They also do things that are intimidating. Self-control also involves learning how to control your behavior when someone tries to intimidate you.

It is absolutely essential that you pay attention to controlling your own reactions. You may not be able to completely control your own anger, but at least you can make sure that you don't communicate your anger in ways that will make the situation worse.

PRINCIPLE 8: WHAT YOU FOCUS ON, YOU GET MORE OF

Here's a principle that applies not only to defusing angry people, but to life in general. It seems like

Bet You Didn't Know

Foreseeable & Unforeseeable Mistakes
Some mistakes are totally unforeseeable, because their negative impact is something that a reasonable person couldn't anticipate. Other mistakes and their impacts are easier to anticipate. For example, take the word "boy". It may be well used to refer to a young person, but we can anticipate that if one used it to refer to a person who has experienced discrimination against those with darker skins, that it would inflame and antagonize. It's foreseeable.

when you focus your attention on something, you get more of it. When people focus on doing work rather than results, they get more work. When people think about food all the time, they tend to eat a lot.

With respect to hostile situations, this principle has a specific application. When a hostile person brings up red herrings that have little to do with the reason you are having the conversation, you have one of two choices. The first is to sidestep the red herring and NOT focus much on it. The second is to "dignify" the red herring by talking about it. If you focus on the red herring, you will encourage the person to talk more about it. When you do NOT focus on it, you are less likely to encourage the person to continue on that theme.

But we have previously stated that it is important to acknowledge the angry and frustrated feelings of a customer. Is this not focusing on something that we don't want more of? Yes and no. The purpose of acknowledging is to show that you are being attentive and understanding, without going into any depth about all the details of the person's feelings or story. That is why the CARP model specifies that after acknowledging, you REFOCUS back to the problem. So you acknowledge and move on. Acknowledge and move on.

PRINCIPLE 9: DON'T SUPPLY AMMUNITION

Lord knows, a hostile person can dredge up enough ammunition by themselves, without your providing the shells to load into the weapon. You can be sure that if you sigh, roll your eyes, show frustration, mutter, or do similar things, that you are reloading the person's weapons. Your words and actions can also be used against you if the customer chooses to lodge a complaint with someone else in the organization For example, when you slam the phone down noisily on an obnoxious customer, what you have done is to encourage the person to complain to someone, and claim that you slammed the phone down, or you were rude. And then you have to explain, and get more frustrated with the situation. You don't need the hassle.

Snapshot

High Gain—High Risk
Simply put high gain, high risk behavior will either work very well, or will badly backfire and make a bad situation much worse. Use with great care.

Things that you say can also be used as ammunition against you and your company. Be aware that some hostile people will try to get you to agree to something, so they can use that agreement as a weapon when talking to another staff member. For example, a person complains to you that Jim, a colleague of yours, gave him the wrong information. Without looking into it you reply *"Well, obviously Jim was mistaken"*. Your customer may very well go back to Jim and quote you or say something like *"Even [your name] thinks you're wrong, your very own staff"*.

See the problem? So, one thing you want to think about is what kinds of things you say and do that might be used in the attack on you, or on another person.

PRINCIPLE 10: DON'T ASK QUESTIONS YOU DON'T WANT TO HEAR ANSWERS TO

Questions are an important tool in defusing, but often employees ask questions when they really do not want to deal with the answers, or spend any time on the answers. The best way to illustrate this is with the following example.

> **Customer:** *It's because I'm green [ethnic background] isn't it. You just **don't like green people**.*
>
> **Employee:** *Why do you think I don't like green people?*
>
> **Customer:** *Isn't it obvious ? I see you giving these non-green people what they want. And I'm the only green person here ... so I'd have to be an idiot not to notice your racist attitudes ... [and on and on].*

The employee wanted to show that she was concerned about the customer's remarks, and wanted the customer to know that he was being taken seriously. Presumably, the idea was that the customer would realize the employee was concerned and would calm down.

Unfortunately, look what happened. The client made an accusation of bias, which we will presume was untrue. The employee, by asking the question, opened the door for more discussion which clearly was not in anyone's best interests. Note also how this fits in with Principle Nine. The employee focused on the accusation of racism, and therefore got more of it.

Now, in some situations, it may be appropriate to ask the above question. It depends on the situation. You need to judge whether there is anything to be gained by asking such a question. If you NEED to ask it, then do so, but be aware that it encourages the client to continue on the topic, rather than on the problem the customer is having in the first place.

PRINCIPLE 11: AVOID INADVERTENT ERRORS

You don't intentionally say things to customers to make them angrier or more hostile, right? Many hostile situations escalate because the employee does not realize that he or she is saying or doing something that doesn't come across as helpful as intended. An example:

> Customer calls asking for Marlene. Marlene is out, so you inform the customer that a message can be left. The customer complains about being given the run-around and how long everything is taking. You inform the person that you will check to see if you can do something for them and put them on hold. It takes you several minutes to find the file. When you get back to the phone, the customer explodes about the wait.

What a surprise! You may have been trying to be helpful, but the customer TOLD you they were angry about the time everything takes. Is it any surprise that they got angrier, having to wait SOME MORE? Not really. <u>You inadvertently made things worse by trying to be helpful in the wrong way.</u>

If you want to get really good at defusing, you need to view your own behavior **AS IT APPEARS** to the customer. It may be that what you think will be helpful, from your perspective, may be seen as negative by the customer. Think like the customer, or put yourself in their position. That can help.

PRINCIPLE 12: AVOID HIGH RISK, HIGH GAIN BEHAVIOR

High risk, high gain behavior is behavior that, when it works, is very effective in defusing. When it doesn't work it escalates the conflict to an extreme degree. For example, telling someone to be quiet may be effective in some situations, and the customer may realize that he is acting inappropriately. But for many people, being told to be quiet is like being told to shut up, and is bound to escalate the situation.

Another example is humor. Humor can be a great technique to defuse a situation, when it works. If you can say something that gets the customer to smile or laugh, you will probably defuse the situation. However if you try humor and the customer doesn't think it's funny, they will think you just aren't taking them seriously. Then they will be really mad. High risk, high gain.

Chapter V - The Art Of Self-Control

INTRODUCTION

For some, the most difficult part of the defusing hostility process is maintaining control over one-self. After all, hostile clients often say things that are personally demeaning or insulting, or their tone of voice may be offensive. If you allow yourself to get angry, and convey that anger to the customer, the situation is more likely to get worse rather than better.

Losing self-control doesn't necessarily mean complete loss of control. Most of the time, employees don't lose control to the point where they swear or yell. Nonetheless it is fairly common for employees to lose ENOUGH control so they make the situation worse. This slight lack of control results in the person using a confrontation tone of voice, or phrases that sound provocative or challenging to the customer. For example, an employee has a particularly unpleasant conversation with a customer. At the end of the conversation, the employee say, in a sarcastic voice *"Have a nice day"*. Or the employee responds to the customer in the same abusive way that the customer uses.

 Bet You Didn't Know

Two Ways To Appear To Maintain Self-Control
With respect to maintaining self-control, the critical part is appearing to the customer like you master your emotional reactions. Two ways: You simply don't GET upset at nasty customer antics OR, you do get upset and you mask it so the customer doesn't get the satisfaction from it. Guess which is best?

In almost all cases, such behavior will create more anger on both sides, and results in the conversation resuming or lasting longer. Even worse, the less self-control exerted, the more likely the conflict will escalate into a dangerous crisis situation.

In this chapter we examine some techniques or tactics to help you "keep your cool" under fire.

 Snapshot

One of the most difficult parts of the defusing hostility process is maintaining control over oneself.. Believe it or not, though, you can work at it. It's much like altering a bad habit, like smoking. Easier probably.

HOW DO WE LOSE SELF-CONTROL?

Every one of us has experienced getting angry, and behaved in angry or hostile ways, so we all have some sense as to how it happens. Still, it's useful to review the pattern.

When we lose a bit of our self-control, we are usually responding to specific things that the other person is saying or doing. We call these things "triggers", though you may be more familiar with the phrase "getting your buttons pushed".

When you get triggered, you tend to react quickly and with little thought - what we call a knee-jerk reaction.

That is why the loss of control is so dangerous. Recall that in an earlier section we mentioned that angry behavior is learned very young, and that when people are under stress, they tend to go back to ways of responding that remain from childhood. These immediate, almost automatic responses are almost always the incorrect ones. This is one situation where your immediate gut reaction is going to get you into trouble.

By acting quickly, you will enter into the escalation cycle, and as both people get angrier, the interaction moves faster and faster, and becomes more intense. As the pace quickens and intensifies, neither party listens.

TACTIC 1: IDENTIFYING YOUR TRIGGERS

Each of us has a set of triggers. You know, those things that just drive us nuts. The interesting thing about your triggers is they are likely to be different from mine, or from your colleagues. And, your triggers are likely to be different with different sets of people. For example, something your spouse does at home may not bother you if a customer does it, or vice versa.

A first step to improve your self-control is to identify the triggering behavior that gets to you. You may find that just by virtue of identifying them, you will get a bit better at avoiding the triggering process.

To help you along, we've listed some common triggers.

Use them stimulate your thinking about your own "hot buttons".

Tone of Voice

- whining
- yelling
- patronizing
- Sarcastic

Specific Words

- certain swear words

Actions

- pounding on desk or counter
- waving arms around
- pointing
- waving finger in face
- putting hand on arm
- ripping up paper
- throwing things
- slamming doors

Content of Comments

- sexist
- racist
- suggestions you are incompetent lazy
  - stupid
  - uncaring
- suggestions other employees are:
  - incompetent
  - lazy
  - uncaring
- accusations that you are racist or biased
- suggestion you don't like the customer
- guilt or blaming attack (It's your fault if...)
- threats (I'll *get you fired*, or, I *have friends*)

TACTIC 2: SLOW DOWN YOUR RESPONSES

Earlier we mentioned that when you get triggered you tend to respond quickly and without thinking, and that these initial responses are usually ineffective ones. One tactic is to learn how to delay your response so that the gut response that comes out so quickly doesn't occur. The reality is that you need a few seconds to think about what you should do, so you can formulate a good response.

You CAN learn how to do this, but it does require some attention and effort. After a while you can get into the habit of not responding immediately.

When you are dealing with a hostile customer, consciously slow your responses down. Remember Grandma's Rule? When you are angry, count to ten before you say anything? Well, you can't count to ten, but you can count to two or three before responding. By doing so, you break the trigger/automatic response cycle, and you will find this will help you keep yourself under control.

Another way of controlling your own response is to take a reasonably deep breath before responding. You need to make sure that when you release the deep breath, that it doesn't come at as a big sigh, as this is annoying to some people.

Count to two or three, and/or take at least one deep breath before responding. Do this consciously at first, and you will find that each time, it becomes easier and more automatic. If you work at it, eventually, it will become a new habit, replacing the automatic, ineffective response to the triggering behavior of the customer.

 Snapshot

Time Outs:
The time out allows you to gather your wits, particularly when facing an unexpected verbal attack, and, if done properly can calm down the customer.

TACTIC 3: BREATHE

This may sound self-evident or even silly, but when under attack by a customer you will be better able to control your own behavior if you make sure you breathe. Breathing is linked to both mental and physical states. Paying attention to your breathing will help you stay relaxed and feel centered. There's a tendency for people under stress to actually stop breathing, and this has the effect of causing the muscles, particularly in the chest, to tense up. Anger is both an emotion ``in the head`` but it also includes a number of physical reactions. Counter the physical actions and you are better able to reduce the effects of the emotion. Breathe.

Tactic 4: Focus/Relax a Body Part

Focusing on, and relaxing a body part is best learned and practiced when you don't need it, so that you get good enough at it to use it when under stress. The technique involves focusing on a body part , say your fingers or a hand, and imagining it getting heavy and warm. Another technique involves consciously tensing the muscles in one hand tight tight, and then letting go all at once. In both cases become aware of the hand and focus on the sensations. By doing this, you "take yourself out of the anger provoking situation", mentally for a very short time. This helps "ground you". It's great if you can couple this with deep breathing. If you choose the hand tensing method, keep the hand out of eyesight of the customer so it doesn't appear like you are clenching your fist with tension or with violent intent.

Tactic 5: Take a time out

When you feel yourself getting upset, or you hear yourself starting to use an impatient tone of voice, arrange for a very brief time out. In many situations, you can take a moment to look for a file, check a regulation, get the customer a cup of coffee, go back to your car for something, etc.

The time out needn't be long at all. In fact, it should be short, since a long wait may inflame some customers. Sometimes even 30 seconds away from the client will be long enough to allow you to take a deep breath or two, and collect yourself. Even a short break can give you the time to remind yourself to stay cool and calm.

Self-talk strategies

In hostile situations, what you say to yourself (self talk) has a large effect on how you feel and what you do. You can make choices regarding your own self talk. For example, when someone is being unpleasant or insulting, your internal dialogue can make it more difficult to maintain self-control. For example, the following examples of self talk are likely to <u>increase</u> your anger:

- I should punch this guy out
- He has some nerve saying...
- Oh, just F*** Off
- Why don't you just go away, a**hole
- Why does this person hate me?
- What did I do to deserve this?
- Ohmygod ... what do I do
- I don't have to put up with this

On the other hand, you can use self talk that is more helpful in terms of maintaining self-control. Positive self talk can help you keep the situation in perspective. For example, you can remind yourself that the person is angry at the situation, not you, or you can remind yourself that the person has a right to be angry. Below are some examples of self talk that are MORE likely to help you maintain self-control.

Snapshot

Positive self-talk can help you keep the situation in perspective. For example, you can remind yourself that the person is angry at the situation, not you. Or you can remind yourself that the person has a right to be angry.

- This person really needs some help
- They aren't really angry at me personally
- I can handle this
- Boy, do they have it rough
- They must look funny naked

The examples in both lists above are just examples. Since each of us is different, you may find that some of the self talk in the first list actually HELPS you maintain control. Or you may find things in the second list that won't work for you. You need to find the self talk statements that work for you, and avoid self talk that doesn't work for you. In the next few sections we are going to look at some examples of self talk that my seminar participants have suggested is effective for them.

TACTIC 6: I'M BETTER THAN THAT

Some people have suggested that they can keep control by reminding themselves that they are "better" than the attacking person, and that they aren't going to stoop to their level. I have found this particular approach very effective for me. Self talk statements such as *"I'm not rolling in the mud with you "*, or *"I won't stoop to that level "* can work very well. Remember this is SELF-TALK. Don't say these things out loud!! This method works well for people who tend to be competitive.

TACTIC 7: I'M NOT GETTING SUCKERED

If you recall, we stated that most of what hostile people say is bait. You can remind yourself of this by saying to yourself "I'm not getting suckered in by your bait", or something similar.

TACTIC 8: I WON'T PAY THE PRICE

Many employees realize that if they respond angrily or lose self-control, they pay the price. When an employee responds

CAUTION!

You WILL Pay
When an employee responds angrily to a customer, it sparks complaints, investigations, and internal hassles that nobody needs. Everyone gets mad at…. YOU! It's not always fair, but it is the reality. You choose.

angrily, it sparks complaints, investigations and internal hassles that nobody needs. But probably more importantly, when we allow ourselves to be triggered, we usually realize we haven't handled the situation well. We may continue to think about the situation for days, feeling embarrassed that we acted badly. So, reminding yourself of these practical outcomes of losing self-control can help.

TACTIC 9: PUT ON THEIR SHOES

One thing you will find is that if you try to understand the client, and why he/she is upset, you are less likely to take the attacks personally. Use self talk that helps you try to understand rather than judge their behavior. Rather than saying to yourself, *"What an idiot"*, try something like *"He must be very frightened to act this way "*, or, *"He must be feeling really desperate "*. This helps remind you that the person is responding more to the situation than you personally.

SECTION SUMMARY

The above tactics and examples can help you design your own self talk to help you maintain control. As with learning to slow your responses down, you will need to work at using new self talk so that you can develop new positive habits to replace the negative ones you might have (and we all have some negative self talk habits).

Being Prepared

You are much more likely to be triggered if you do not expect attacking behavior from a client. Probably the most difficult situations to deal with occur when the attack comes out of the blue -- when you don't expect it. This means that it is important that you both observe and prepare for hostile interactions before they start. Your goal is to try to see these situations coming.

TACTIC 10: OBSERVING

A good part of the time, an observant person can tell that a person approaching them is already agitated or angry, even before anything has been said. Body language is a good indicator, and as the conversation starts, tone of voice and words used will tell you that this person may be difficult to work with.

Whenever possible we want to observe the customer, preferably as they approach us or we approach them. We are looking for signals that the individual is uncomfortable or upset. Some things to look for:

- clenched fists
- fidgetiness when waiting
- glancing at watch
- muscle tension in face

- darting gaze

When the customer says his/her first words, pay special attention to the tone. These first words are very valuable in determining the emotional state of the person.

One thing to remember. Since each person is different in terms of how they look and talk when they are uncomfortable, be aware that the nonverbal behavior you observe may mean nothing at all. Some people are always fidgety, or always look tense, even when they are not. You just want to be prepared in a positive way, and to anticipate POSSIBLE problems.

CAUTION!

You are much more likely to be triggered if you do not expect attacking behavior from a client. Probably the most difficult situations to deal with occur when the attack comes out of the blue, when you don't expect it.

TACTIC 11: PREPARATORY SELF-TALK

Observing is pretty useless unless you can use that information to prepare yourself for potential difficulties. That's where additional self talk comes in. When you observe someone you think may turn hostile, try some of the following self talk phrases:

- I can handle this
- I need to make a special effort to defuse
- I will remain calm and cool

What you need to avoid is any negative self talk that will make you less able to deal with the person effectively. Examples of negative self talk are:

CAUTION!

Humor:
Don't do anything in front of clients or management that might be misunderstood. If you use humor, do it privately, and only with people who understand that it is simply a way of reducing stress levels so you can do an even better job.

- Oh no
- I hope he/she goes somewhere else
- Is it coffee break time?
- There goes the morning

In addition, when you see an upset person approaching, or hear some indicators that the person is angry, remind yourself that you must start defusing immediately. In the next chapter, we will discuss some tactics for starting off interactions effectively. If you observe, prepare positively, and use these initial techniques you will increase your success rate.

General Stress Management Issues

A number of people have asked me if I have any suggestions regarding carryover effects. In other words, if you deal with one hostile customer, how do you avoid letting it affect how you deal with the next person, who may be pleasant.

Another question people ask is how they can deal with hostile people without experiencing a lot of stress and burn out.

This last question is an important one because dealing with upset people all the time is tiring. The answers can be found in the area of stress management. While we can't go into much detail here, we can make the following observations.

Our feelings of stress are related to lifestyle. If we eat well, sleep, exercise, and take care of ourselves, we are less likely to feel stressed, or to burn out. That means that lifestyle IS important. There are a number of good books on the subject that can help you with stress management, and also seminars available on the subject. You may want to investigate these resources.

The first question about carry-over is no less important. We don't want to take out our frustration on the next customer we face. Let's look at a few tactics that people use.

Also remind yourself of any techniques that you may want to use.

Tactic 12: Private Humor

Humor allows us to put things in perspective. As someone once said, *"If I didn't laugh, I'd cry"*. Here are some ways that people use humor to reduce their stress, and get ready for the next client. Keep in mind that you should never use humor to defuse yourself unless you are completely out of view and hearing of ALL customers. Consider also what reaction someone might have — say the CEO of your company, if she observes you giving the finger to someone, albeit on the phone so the customer can't see it.

- making obscene gestures while talking to angry customer on phone
- making faces to co-worker as client rants over the phone
- making humorous comments about client to co-worker **after interaction** with customer is over and nobody can over hear. (e.g. "What a bozo")
- Making fun of customer while he or she is on hold.

Venter or Non-Venter
Most people believe that they need to let out the "steam" inside of them when they are frustrated, or they will blow up, but that's hardly a universal truth. In fact, for many people it works the other way. For them, the more they focus on what has or is being done to them, the more they work themselves up into an emotional frenzy. They obsess.

You don't need to visit a "shrink" to find out whether you are better off if you vent, or better off if you distract yourself instead. Pay attention to what happens when you focus on the nasty stuff the customer is doing, as compared to leaving it behind.

Now, you have to use your head here. Don't do anything in front of clients or even management that might be misunderstood. If you use humor, do it privately, and only with people who understand that it is simply a way of reducing stress levels so you can do an even better job.

TACTIC 13: VENTING / NOT VENTING – THAT IS THE QUESTION

Dealing with hostile customers is frustrating. For many people, this frustration builds and builds, like a pressure cooker, until it bursts. Some people believe it 'is important not to let the pressure build, but to "vent" it out, by talking to co-workers, or other sympathetic people. We call the process of talking out our frustration, venting.

You are probably familiar with it, and already use it. But venting doesn't work for everyone.

Some people have learned to let go of their frustration by talking it out. They let the steam out, and then things are OK, and they move on to the next situation they must deal with. For them, venting works.

For others, focusing on their frustration doesn't make it go away but intensifies the frustration. By paying more attention to it, they make the frustration and stress bigger.

You need to figure out which type of person you are. If you find that you vent, only to return to the situation later, you may benefit by not venting. In other words, if you vent, then leave the issue, then vent a few hours later, then return to the issue and so on, the venting is probably not working for you.

If venting doesn't work for you, you can try a distraction technique. If focusing on the problem person makes you angrier and angrier you need to do things that will get your mind off the situation or person. If you are at home after a bad day, rather than sitting around thinking about it, or talking on and on about it, do something different. Watch a movie, play a computer game, exercise, or do whatever will allow you to stop thinking about the unpleasant event.

For some people not venting is better. For some distracting and moving on works well.

Chapter Conclusion

In this chapter we have talked about tactics for self-control and a bit about stress management. Remember that you need to find out what works for YOU. I have provided some suggestions, many passed on to me from customer service staff who work "on the line", so you can use them to come up with solutions that fit your style and personality.

This page left blank intentionally

Chapter VI- Starting Off Successfully

INTRODUCTION

Here are some key points from previous chapters:

- It is much easier to defuse hostility before the person gets up a good head of steam. You save more time, and get less aggravated.
- If you come across as a real human being, rather than a piece of the bureaucratic machinery, you are less likely to receive hostility.
- It is important to observe and prepare so you are ready to deal with a potentially angry and hostile client.
- It is important to prevent the hostile customer from taking control of the conversation.

In this chapter we are going to talk about some approaches you can take to properly interact with your customers so you reduce the odds of the customer becoming angrier.

TACTIC 14: GREETING

Whether you deal with customers in person or on the phone, the way you begin a conversation will affect how the customer treats you. You know what they say -- first impressions are hard to change. If the other person concludes you are cold, distant, bored, uninterested, uncaring or unhelpful, their level of anger will escalate almost immediately. Customers develop these perceptions very quickly.

Project a positive image, as the customer approaches you, or in the first few sentences of the conversation. Just as important, take control of the conversation early. Finally, you want your customer to know that you recognize them as an individual, and not just another customer. Bet you didn't realize the greeting was quite so important.

Snapshot

Whether you deal with customers in person or on the phone, the way you begin a conversation will affect how the customer treats you. You DO have influence even if it seems you don't.

You can do this by using appropriate greetings when a customer approaches you, or when you answer the phone.

An effective greeting includes:

- Appropriate nonverbal behavior
- Eye contact
- Posture that indicates interest

- Appropriate tone of voice
  - Friendly
  - Calm
  - Efficient sounding

- Appropriate Content
  - Offer/Commitment to help
  - Acknowledgment
  - Effective timing

EYE CONTACT

When you deal with a client, it is important to look at the person when you greet them. A common error made by busy people is not looking at the customer as he approaches. This isn't intentional, but it does give the impression that the customer is not an individual. It feels like you are treating the person as an object and that increases aggression.

We will talk about eye contact in a later chapter, but for now, be aware that you want to make eye contact via glances and not by staring.

POSTURE

Your nonverbal language conveys whether you are interested in the customer or not. If you look bored, the customer will perceive you as too distant. When greeting a customer consider leaning forward slightly. This is a standard posture of interest, whether you are standing or sitting.

CAUTION!

A common error made by people is that they don't look at the person as they approach. This isn't intentional, but it does give the impression that the customer is not an individual, but just another task to perform. That increases aggression.

Most people realize that a smile is an effective technique in a greeting, and for the most part it is. Except when it's obviously fake. No smile is better than a phony smile (we call a phony smile a "gleep"). If you have a miserable day, and feel wretched, what happens if you force a smile? The customer will know its not real, and falseness encourages aggression.

Finally, smiling must be appropriate. If your job is to inform people of tragedies affecting their families, a big smile used as greeting is clearly inappropriate.

TONE OF VOICE

Tone of voice may be the most important part of greeting a customer. Sound interested, even if you are harried or very busy. Remember that if you sound upset, the customer will assume you are upset at him, even though this may not be the case.

Don't sound like Mr. Rogers, though. Your tone of voice can be professional, and show interest without sounding disgustingly sugar coated. Keep in mind that appropriateness is everything. Fit your tone to the job, the customer's demeanor on approach, and the situation. For example, a customer who has been waiting for 45 minutes to see you wants you to sound efficient and fast, not cheery and chatty.

CONTENT

An effective greeting makes clear that you are there to help, and may also contain something like *"Good morning"* or *"Hello "*. Except for acknowledgments that may be required, it is wise to keep your greeting short, and to the point IF THE CLIENT IS APPROACHING YOU. In other words, don't begin a conversation by talking about all kinds of extraneous topics. After all, when a customer comes to you, they are usually coming because they need more than social chit-chat.

Here's an interesting thing, though. The amount of chit-chat and social interaction that is appropriate between you and a customer is going to be partly determined by the geographic area in which you live, and the size of the city in which you live. For example, if you are in New York, a less chatty (but very fast) interaction is more likely to be successful compared to a small town in North Dakota. There are regional differences in most large countries, between rural and urban, and between small and large places. Stay alert to these differences, and also to differences in preferences that have to do with industries. Should a plumber be as sociable as a restaurant employee? Things to think about.

In the situation where you approach the customer on his or her own turf — let's say if you do home repairs, or service office equipment, you may want to spend a little more time creating a sense of trust and rapport with the customer. That doesn't mean you will yap about irrelevant things all day, but you might spend a bit more time building rapport. (see Tactic 15).

ACKNOWLEDGMENT

The second exception to the *"Good morning, what can I do for you today"* short greeting occurs when you notice the person is already upset or angry. Since you are observing and preparing for customers, you will see behaviors such as fidgetiness, looking at watch, scowling, etc. When you see these things, it should be a signal that you need to expand your greeting by acknowledging the person's state or situation.

For example, George works at a front office counter. He sees that the customer approaching him has been waiting for several minutes and seems upset by the wait. The customer keeps looking at his watch.

Just as the customer approaches the counter, George begins:

George: Good morning, <u>I bet you're in a hurry?</u> So what can I do for you?

Customer: Damn right I'm in a hurry, why does it always take so long?

George: Just lots of people, but what can I do to get you done quickly.

Customer: *Well, I need...*

Notice that George greets and then acknowledges the person is in a hurry (underlined portion). You will also notice that George avoids any lengthy discussion of how long things are taking. Again, you have an example of acknowledging AND refocusing on the issue (CARP model).

EFFECTIVE TIMING

Timing is critical in the greeting. You want to be the first one to speak, and including a question will encourage the customer to respond to you from square one. This is a control tactic. By speaking first, and not giving the person an opportunity to seize control from the beginning, you can reduce abusive behavior.

So, don't hesitate. If you work at a counter or situation where the customer approaches you, you can begin your greeting even before the person stops moving towards you. You want to speak first.

 Wise Thoughts To Ponder

Emotion and Rapport
Usually, the more emotional the customer is, the more time you may need to spend creating some rapport and interacting on a human to human level.

TACTIC 15: GENERATING RAPPORT

When a client approaches you, your greeting should be short and to the point. Sometimes, it is more appropriate to spend a bit of time in conversation before getting down to business. We call this generating rapport.

What we mean by this is that you spend a minute or two asking questions or talking on subjects other than the reason for the conversation. It's about relationship building, or in the case of an existing relationship, it's about maintaining a positive relationship.

There are two situations where this is particularly appropriate. One is when you approach the customer. The second is when you have worked with the client before. Let's look at two examples:

Colleen works as a health inspector visiting restaurants. Her job is to look for health and safety violations. Not surprisingly, many people are not overly pleased to see her. She enters a restaurant and approaches the manager/owner, Mr. Jasper. She has met him several times before (relationship already exists).

> **Colleen:** Good morning Mr. Jasper. How are you today? I hope you've been getting some of the convention business this month?

Jasper: Ya, it's been OK.

Colleen: It's nice to see restaurants like yours doing well. I guess you know why I'm here. I need to take a look for the usual health and safety issues, but you've always done well in the past.

Jasper: OK, where would you like to start?

In the example, note that Colleen asks a question about business, showing that she is interested. This is a simple way to generate rapport -- ask a greeting question about something you know is important to the client, and is likely to be a positive thing to talk about.

By the way, if this had been Colleen's first visit, she would also have had to introduce herself and provide some information to the manager. She still might have asked some rapport building questions like:

So, how have the first few months been in the business?

Been very busy?

In the next example, the employee and the customer have worked together before. Mr. Smith, the customer, comes into the office at least once a month. Janet Wilson, the employee, has helped the customer before, but also knows that Mr. Smith is often annoyed or hostile. Janet handles the greeting like this:

Janet: Good morning, Mr. Smith. I hope you got your problem from last month sorted out .. how did that work out?

Mr. Wilson: Well, I didn't get what I wanted, but at least I spoke to your boss.

Janet: Well, at least you had your say. What can I do for you today ?

In this example, Janet refers to the last time she met with the client. This shows he is important enough to remember, and expresses interest. It helps create rapport so that Mr. Wilson is less likely to be hostile.

TACTIC 16: USING NAMES

People like to hear their own names. Likewise, they like to know your name. The use of names helps both parties see each other as real people, and as unique individuals. When possible you want to use the person's name as early as you can. You probably want to give your name, if that is appropriate.

Just a few notes on using names. Things aren't always simple, even with names.

Snapshot
People like to hear their own names. Likewise, they like to know your name. The use of names helps both parties see each other as real people, and as unique individuals.

With people you haven't met before use the more formal Mr./Mrs./Miss/Ms. form. This is more respectful. If you don't know which one to use ask. For example, "Do you prefer Mrs. or Ms.?"

If you have worked with a person previously, and want to set a less formal tone to the conversation, first names can be useful. However, some people won't like this.

If you don't know if it's OK to use first names, ask. Try: "Do you prefer I call you Mr. Smith, or is John OK? " or "If you like you can call me Bob, how would you like to be addressed? "

When giving your name out, consider security issues. Some organizations don't like staff to give out their last names. If you work with potentially unbalanced or very hostile, violent clientele, first names may be best.

CHAPTER CONCLUSION

We have discussed a few tactics for beginning potentially hostile interactions in an effective way. What we want to do is to convey helpfulness while recognizing the customer as an individual, and building rapport as necessary. Also, the greeting stage is when you begin to exert control over the conversation by being proactive.

Chapter VII — The Art Of Cooperative Language

INTRODUCTION

Have you noticed that some words and phrases sound confrontational and challenging, while others sound more cooperative and calming? You may not have thought about it before, but you automatically use different kinds of language in different situations. For example, when you talk with your boss, you probably alter the words, phrases and tone of voice so you communicate differently then when you talk to your children. If you don't alter the way you speak in different situations, you are likely to be a poor communicator who is often frustrated. Being responsive to the communication context — who you are speaking with, and how you are speaking is the key to more harmonious relationships.

Snapshot

The way you phrase things when talking to an angry customer affects the reaction you get. You can sound arrogant, disbelieving, mistrustful, challenging, and uncaring, or you can sound cooperative, willing to listen and discuss, and be flexible.

So, here's the problem. While we are taught how to be "nice", we don't learn skills that are specific enough or learned well enough to allow us to communicate effectively when things get difficult. We make mistakes because we miss a lot of the subtle things that make the difference between communicating in cooperative ways, and communicating in ways that annoy or anger. The more stress we feel, and the more we become upset, angry or hurt, the more likely we are to forget to modify our communication. We "let it fly", so to speak.

When we do that, we make the situation worse.

No doubt you understand that your tone and voice qualities convey lots of underlying messages that can make a sentence sound pleasant, or make the same sentence sound nasty, even though the words spoken are the same. However, the words and phrases themselves **are** important. Some ways of saying things are calming, and some are inflammatory just because of the word choices we make.

In this chapter we are going to talk about two different types of language, and the importance of using cooperative and calming language when dealing with hostile customers. In addition, we will talk about a few other language related techniques that can be used with hostile customers.

TYPE 1 & TYPE 2 LANGUAGE

The way you phrase things to hostile customers affects their reactions. You can sound arrogant, disbelieving, mistrustful, challenging, and uncaring, or you can sound cooperative, willing to listen, and discuss, while also conveying flexibility. The unfortunate thing is that if you are not aware of the ways you use language, you may inadvertently SOUND confrontational, even if you don't mean to be. It is important to be aware of how you phrase things, so you won't accidentally make hostile situations worse. The idea is to become more observant of and in control of the language choices you make.

TYPE 1 LANGUAGE - CONFRONTATIONAL LANGUAGE

Type 1 language is language that sends the following messages:

- you are absolutely certain you are right
- you are unwilling to consider the other person's position
- challenges the other person to back up what they say
- has a harsh, confrontational tone
- the other person has no choices
- the customer is to blame
- the customer does not have 'an out'

 Bet You Didn't Know

We Really Do Know
Everyone learns at a very young age how to use words to get their way and manipulate, because children are very self-centered. We also tend to "remember" how to get cooperation, when it's pointed out to us, as is done in this book. We really do know, but we don't realize we know. Now you are better able to think about language in a different way to control how you use it.

How does Type 1 language affect the other person's behavior? When you use Type I language you tend to encourage the customer to also use confrontational language. This generally causes the situation to escalate, as each of you increases the force and energy used in the conversation.

This kind of language also gives the impression of lack of choice for the customer, something we have talked about earlier as contributing to a sense of desperation, helplessness and frustration on the part of the customer. They become harder to work with.

TYPE 2 LANGUAGE COOPERATIVE LANGUAGE

Type 2 language is at the opposite end. It sends completely different messages, messages more likely to help the customer realize that you are trying to work with him or her. Specifically, cooperative language conveys that::

- you are willing to consider other person's position
- you recognize you COULD be wrong (but not likely)
- invites person to discuss rather than challenges
- has a milder, cooperative tone
- leaves room for choice
- tends to blame nobody
- helps customer save face

- focuses on future rather than the past

How does Type 2 language affect the customer? The customer realizes that you DO care about him or her and that you really do want to help. The customer realizes you are trying to work WITH them, and want to be on the same side, to help deal with the problem, or make the best of a bad situation. It takes difficult situations from a "you" versus "customer" to one where you are working towards some common goals.

The best way to get a feel for the two kinds of language is to look at some examples of each. Consider the following phrases:

1. *We always send out this information to customers.*

2. *That's impossible. I would never have done that.*

3. *Didn't you even read the menu?*

 Wise Thoughts To Ponder

Are these Type 1 or Type 2? Look at each sentence. Sentence (1) implies that what the client is saying is impossible. It implies the customer MUST be wrong , and that the customer is probably to blame for the problem EVEN IF THAT'S not said explicitly. It suggests you might think the customer is lying or stupid. How can a wasteful argument not occur as a result?

Small Change, Huge Impact
It's absolutely an amazing experience when you discover that tiny changes in the words and tone you use can have such a huge impact on the reactions of another human being.

Sentence (2) uses the word <u>always,</u> a common word in Type I language. The use of "always" implies that we never make mistakes, and suggests that if something has gone wrong, it is the customer's fault. It's a blaming statement, again, indirectly, but that's what is "between the lines". Same result.

Sentence (3) is the most blatant part of the response. It uses a question in a way that is challenging, and implies the person may not be very smart, or that you think the customer is lazy. Certainly it suggests that the customer is to blame.

These are all confrontational. Fine if you actually want to spend 30 minutes arguing, getting angry and insulted, while accomplishing nothing.

Can we change the words so the employee sounds more cooperative? Sure. Let's take a look at the first (1) sentence above. We can substitute Type 2 language as follows. These are ALL better.

- *It's odd you didn't receive the information.*
- *We usually send out this information to claimants.*
- *Perhaps it's just gotten lost somewhere.*

Look at what we changed. In sentence (1), the speaker expresses some surprise at the situation, in a way that doesn't suggest the customer is lying, or to blame. It INVITES reasonable discussion without trying to pin responsibility on the customer's rear end.

Sentence (2) is only slightly altered, with the word <u>usually</u> used instead of *always*. The word "always" is absolute, while the word "usually" sends a more gentle message. A tiny change of one word completely alters the meaning of the sentence, and completely alters the reaction you will get.

Words like sometimes, perhaps, often, are called language softeners, because they make what is said sound less harsh. Not wishy washy, just less harsh.

Finally, sentence (3) begins with the word "**perhaps**", another less absolute word, and suggests that it is possible that the material has gotten lost, without pointing the finger at the customer. No blame. No pain.

Let's look at a second example of phrases:

1. *Sir, There is no point arguing with me.*

2. *You have to lodge your appeal with our Customer Service Department*

What do you think? Cooperative or confrontational language?

In sentence (1) the speaker uses the wording, " *There is no point*", which is an absolute statement. It's harsh. In sentence (2), the speaker uses the words "*You have to*" which implies no choice, and sounds like a command rather than a helpful suggestion. Do YOU like being ordered around by some stranger? Of course not. It causes backlash.

It's absolutely critical to understand that truth can be expressed cooperatively and in a helping manner, or it can be expressed in a confrontational way. The sentences above may be true. There probably IS no point in arguing with you. It may be the case that the individual WILL have to lodge a complaint with the customer service department. Can we express the same "truth" in a way that isn't inflammatory? Sure we can.

OK, let's fix it with the following phrases:

1. *Sir, I don't think I can help you with this but I know just the person who might be able to help.*

2. *If you want to pursue it, the best thing is to contact our Customer Service Department.*

3. *Would you like the contact information?*

This Type 2 response has almost the same content but sounds more helpful and cooperative.

Sentence (1) suggests the employee doesn't think he can help. Notice, he didn't say *"I can't help you "*, or *"I won't help you"*, which are more absolute statements. The employee uses phrasing that sounds flexible and helpful — verbal softeners.

In sentence (2) the speaker starts off with the word "if", suggesting that the customer has a choice, rather than sounding like the employee is ordering the customer around. And, in sentence (3), rather than giving the information to the customer directly, the employee shows respect by asking if they would like the information, again providing choice while appearing helpful.

Inflammatory Type 1 (Confrontational language)	Replace With Type 2 (Cooperative) language
I can't	I don't think I can
We never …	We don't usually…
We (I) always …	• We (I) try to … • We (I) usually …
You must have … (lost it)	It's possible that …
You must …	• The best thing to do is … • Have you thought about …? • You might try … • If you like, you can …
That's impossible	That hardly ever happens here
You can't	I don't think that's going to help you
You were … (speeding)	Are you aware that you were speeding?
Don't	It might be better if you … (state positive option)
You're wrong	Is it possible that …?
You have a problem	We have a problem here
You should have …	If you …, then you will …

Hopefully these examples help you understand the difference between the two kinds of language. To help you further, we have provided a table of phrases and words that tend to be associated with the two types of language. Take a look at the table above. Look at them carefully. See if you can add to the list of both confrontational language and cooperative language.

Tactic 17: Appropriate Use of Type 1 & Type 2 Language

By now, it may have occurred to you that there may be situations where Type 1 language is AP-PROPRIATE and even desirable. While we recommend that you use as much Type 2 cooperative language as much as possible, there may be occasions where the stronger and more challenging Type 1 language is appropriate.

The key is being able to assess the situation, and your customer, to determine if you should switch to Type 1 language. The general rule is to stick with Type 2, until it is clear that stronger statements are needed. Then switch to Type 1 only long enough to gain control of the interaction, then move back to Type 2. Again, you know your clients best, so use your own judgment. Remember that the more aggressive you become, the higher the risk.

Let's continue to look at other ways you can convey positive constructive messages to your disappointed or angry customers.

Tactic 18: Use of WE

Snapshot

We = "Same Side"
Something you want to do is give the impression that you are working with the client, not against them. You may find that replacing the words 'you' and 'I' with WE can give the impression you are on the same side as the client. It suggests cooperation.

You want to give the impression that you are working WITH the client, not against her. You may find that replacing the words "you" and "I" with WE can give the impression you are on the same side as the client. It suggests cooperation.

Be careful not to overuse "We" in a conversation. Pick your spots so the use of *We* makes sense. For example, it is non-sensical to say to someone *"Well, Sir, we need to fill out our forms before they can be processed. "* This sounds patronizing, and sounds like you are speaking to a child. Not good.

However, if a customer calls, or comes in complaining that you have incorrect information about her, it may be appropriate to say:

"I guess <u>we'd</u> better take a look at that". "

"Let's see what <u>we</u> can do about that".

Tone & Word Stress

As indicated earlier establishing a cooperative climate involves more than the words you use. It also involves using the appropriate tone of voice for the situation. For example, you can say *"Have a nice day"* in a way that tells the customer to get stuffed, or in a way that indicates that you mean what you say. It depends on the WAY you say it, and the context.

In a book of this sort, it is difficult to deal with tone of voice and word stress, since you can't hear what I am writing. However we can give you some suggestions about monitoring your tone of voice and matching it to the situation.

TACTIC 19: USING APPROPRIATE TONE & WORD STRESS

First, some information. Cooperative tones of voice have one characteristic in common. When a person speaks in a calm, cooperative way, he usually stresses only one or two words in a sentence. When we talk about stress, we are referring to verbal emphasis on words. When a person speaks in an angry, frustrated or confrontational way, he usually stresses more words in each sentence.

 Bet You Didn't Know

It IS The Words
One of the best things you can do to prevent conflict, not only with customers, but with colleagues, friends and family is to pay attention to the nuances and subtleties of the language you use. Hot words, hot phrases and "less than" language is common place, and often used without malice but they create anger in others.

To help you "hear" the difference let's look at the sentence below.

I'm not going to help you unless you lower your voice.

Now, we will mark the emphasized words by capitalizing them. First, a hostile pattern:

Say this to yourself, or better yet, say it out loud, as if you are angry. Which words are you emphasizing or stressing?

If you are like many other people, this is how you would say it:

> *I'm **NOT** going to **HELP** you unless **YOU** lower your **VOICE**.*

You may have emphasized different words, but the point is that you will likely have at least four heavily stressed words.

Now, let's look at the same sentence, but said in a cooperative tone. Imagine that you are calm, not feeling any anger what so ever. Now, say this sentence to yourself, once again:

> *I'm not going to help you unless you lower your voice.*

Did you emphasize fewer words. Probably. This is one way you could have emphasized the words:

> I'm not going to **HELP YOU** unless you lower your voice.

Can you hear the difference?

You can become more aware of the tone you use by practicing listening to yourself speak. This is a little tricky to master, but if you listen to others, and listen to yourself when you speak, you'll get a better feel about how to remove the extra emphasized words to reduce the feeling of aggression.

HOT PHRASES & WORDS

In the previous section, we mentioned that **even if the content of what** you say is cooperative, a non-cooperative tone of voice will "drown" the positive content of your message. But the opposite can occur. There are some words and phrases that have such emotional meaning for people so that no matter how nice your tone of voice may be, the customer will hear what you say as insulting or inflammatory. We use the term **hot phrases**, or hot words, to refer to language which should be avoided.

My favorite examples of hot phrases/words are:

- *I don't care....*
- *Whatever*

There is no way that you can use either of these and sound cooperative and helpful. It just can't be done. If you have ever had someone say *"Whatever"*, to you, you know how aggravating it can be. Same with *"I don't care"* What happens is that the other person hears these words, and because they have an emotional effect, they tend not to hear what else you say. For example, you say:

> *I don't care if you DID send in your application. I want to help you fill out this new one so you can get your insurance check.*

What does the customer hear?

> *I don't care blah blah blah wallawalla bing bang.*

And they don't like it. Off you go down the path to an argument by accident.

TACTIC 20: AVOID HOT WORDS & PHRASES

Simply, you want to avoid hot phrases and words. We have provided a list of hot phrases and words that should generally be avoided. Take a look at them after you have examined Tactic 21, below.

TACTIC 21: AVOID REPEATING HOT WORDS & PHRASES

Hostile customers use a lot of hot words and phrases in their verbal attacks. They may call you stupid, incompetent, an idiot, or accuse you of being racist, or corrupt, or lazy or ... well you get the idea.

In the CARP model we suggest that you need to acknowledge the person's upset and situation. What you DON'T want to do is repeat the hot words that the customer uses. For example:

Customer: *You wouldn't treat me this way if I wasn't "green", you just don't like green people.*

Employee: *Your race doesn't affect how I treat you. We deal with lots of green people here.*

The employee has made several mistakes here, not the least is responding to this attack with a defensive statement. Apart from that, the employee uses the word *"race"* which is a hot word, and repeats the word *"green"*. Most words connected with ethnic background are hot, so this is a mistake, and likely to cause the conflict to escalate. Repeating hot phrases focuses attention on what you don't want, and you just get more of it.

CAUTION!

Beware The "Why" Question
Questions are a powerful way to invite people into constructive dialogue. However, they can be misused so it sounds like you are interrogating the person. "Why" questions are most likely to annoy because they are perceived as challenging. Poorly phrases "why" questions can cause the other person to become defensive. Proper tone and word stresses are critical to make it work.

So, you may ask: How do I respond to this type of thing?
There are always non hot words that mean about the same thing. These you can use. So the employee could have said:

> "Your *BACKGROUND* doesn't affect how I treat you. We deal with people from *EVERY WALK OF LIFE.*"

In this example, the employee has removed the hot words. It still isn't a great response because it dignifies the attack, and focuses on it, but it is a good example of how you can replace hot words with non-hot phrases.

We will come back to this in the next chapter when we discuss verbal self-defense techniques. At this point, take a look at the list of hot words and phrases we have provided.

USING QUESTIONS

The final cooperative language approach involves replacing harder sounding statements with questions. If you have ever been stopped by a police officer for speeding, like as not, one of the first things they did was to ask you a question or two. A common one is *"Do you know how fast you were going?"*, or a variation, *'Are you aware of how fast you were going?"* Why do they do this? There are three reasons. Questions are less likely to provoke a person if they are phrased in this manner. Second, asking a question or two at the beginning allows the officer to assess your state ... do you sound stable, do you sound upset, do you sound intoxicated.

The third reason has to do with control. By asking you the question, the officer is asserting control over the interaction, and encouraging you to respond to him/her.

You can use questions in this manner, too.

Tactic 22: Replace Some Statements With Questions

Asking questions helps you in your ability to control the interaction, shows you are interested in the person, and may help you gather information that will help you with the substance of the person's problem. Questions can be used to replace some statements, so that what you have to say is perceived as more cooperative.

It is important to use a very calm, quiet voice when questioning, so the questioning doesn't sound like an inquisition.

Some examples:

Rather than: "It's not our policy to handle complaints. Go to the manager's office at the back of the store if you want to complain. "

Try: "Did you know that you can speak to our manager to voice your concerns? "

Rather than: "We require you to conform to our policies which are posted by each cash register. "

Try : "Were you aware that we have some policies in place so all of our customers get a fair deal?"

Notice the last example. It allows the customer to say they were not aware of the policies. This gives them a **face saving way** of explaining why they have not followed the regulations. We know that allowing people an out to save face will help stop some long arguments.

Examples of Hot Phrases & Words

- Any reference to specific ethnic backgrounds or race, color, etc. e.g.. Black, Chinese, Ukrainian
- Other words related to unequal treatment, e.g.:
  - racist
  - discrimination
  - bias
  - bigoted
  - race

- Words or phrases that suggest disinterest.
  - Whatever
  - I don't care
  - I don't give a damn
  - That has nothing to do with...
  - I'm not interested in...
  - I don't want to hear about your...

- Phrases that blame or imply blame, or suggest ignorance, e.g.:
    - If you paid attention, you would ...
    - Why don't you listen.
    - You don't know anything about ...
    - Obviously, you haven't...

- Absolute words, e.g.:
    - Always
    - Never

- Phrases that express an opinion about the client
    - I don't like you
    - You are rude
    - You have no right to...

- Phrases that suggest helplessness
    - There's nothing I can do
    - There's nothing you can do

- Phrases that have a threatening undertone, e.g.:
    - If you don't be quiet I will throw you out.
    - You aren't going to get much help if you insult me.

- Phrases that are challenging, e.g.:

    - Go ahead, try to get me fired.
    - Prove to me that you mailed the payment
    - You can do whatever you like, but…
    - My supervisor is going to say the same thing.

This page left blank intentionally

Chapter VIII — Verbal Self-Defense Techniques

In this chapter we present a number of tactics you can use to gain and maintain control over hostile interactions and to turn around awkward conversations.

Introduction

Verbal self defense techniques refer to things you can say — statements or questions you can use to interrupt a hostile person's verbal attacks, and turn around angry conversations almost instantly. They are based on some of the same self defense principles you find in the martial arts, and take into account the nature of angry interactions.

Our primary goal in using self-defense techniques is to regain control of the interaction.. A hostile person tends to hold the floor by not responding to normal questions and continuing to talk and interrupt. We want to stop the person in their tracks, so that they will begin to respond to our questions, and so we can use the rest of the **CARP** model.

 Bet You Didn't Know

The Speed of Verbal Self Defense
One of the great things about using verbal self defense techniques is the speed at which they create positive results. When they work, and of course nothing works all the time, the effect is instantaneous. Control of the conversation returns to you, which means that you can acknowledge the person's feelings and refocus on what you can do to help.

Before we go on to talk about the specific tactics, let's review a few principles from past chapters, and explain a few new ones.

REVIEW

1. The hostility attack game is learned very young. Verbal attackers have developed attack scripts that require little thought to execute.
2. The hostility attack game has "rules". The attacker expects you to respond to attacks in the following ways:
   - Defend (I, We statements)
   - Counterattack (You) statements
3. The attacker wants you to respond to bait, allowing him or her to control your behavior. The best way to stop an attack and reassert control is to avoid playing the game according to the attacker's rules.
4. We need to avoid defensive statements and counterattacking, since these tactics are part of the game the attacker knows well. When we defend or counterattack, the attacker need not stop to think, since he/she has automatic scripts that can be used to continue the attack.

Self-Defense Principles

If you have had any martial arts training, you will probably be familiar with the two principles of self defense we are going to share with you.

The first is **surprise**. When you do what is expected, the opponent is prepared and can act almost without thinking. Whether it be physical self-defense or verbal self-defense, you want to do things that are surprising or unexpected, so that the attacker must pause and think. If you can freeze the opponent in thought or confusion, you create an opening to use other techniques. While you may be aware that this applies to physical attacks, it also applies to verbal attacks.

We want to surprise and confuse and we want to do that in a way that is, in effect, not obvious to the customer.

The second principle relates to how you handle the momentum of the attacker. When a physical attacker throws a punch, he or she develops forward momentum. Their whole body moves forward.

In the martial arts, you are instructed to use that momentum to your advantage. Rather than standing straight up to take the force of a blow, you may take hold of the arm, and use the momentum of the attacker to slip the blow, moving the attacker past you, and forcing the attacker off balance.

You don't want to absorb the force of the blow, but you try to use the attacker's force to your advantage.

The same principle applies to verbal self defense. You don't want to absorb the force of the verbal attack (e.g.. by arguing, defending).

TACTIC 23: USE SURPRISE

If you want to confuse the verbal attacker long enough to use other techniques, and get the attacker to start responding to you, use unexpected, surprising and novel statements and questions. When you do this, it causes the attacker to stop and think. Usually that means that she stops talking or ranting long enough for you to gain control.

If you want to use the element of surprise to gain control of an interaction, **make sure that the customer does not see your action as demeaning, or indicating a lack of interest** or lack of concern. Remember our earlier example where humor was used? In that example the customer suggested the employee could "Take his forms and stick them where the sun don't shine."

The employee responded with "I would love to oblige you on that, but unfortunately, I have five file folders, six other forms and a large filing cabinet up there, and quite honestly, I don't think that there is room for much more. "

The customer was surprised, paused, and then began laughing. As a result the employee was able to regain control, and went on to use acknowledgment, refocusing and problem-solving techniques.

In this real life example, the humor/surprise tactic worked effectively. However, it could easily have escalated the situation if it hadn't been said in an appropriate tone of voice.

Not all unexpected responses are high risk, high gain. You can use other surprise tactics that are not as "high risk, high gain" as the one in the example. Humor is often unexpected, but carries a high risk. The trick when using humor is to be self-effacing, and show yourself as a human being.

The next set of tactics describe responses that are surprising, and do not carry the same risks associated with humor.

TACTIC 24: THE WHEN QUESTION

Let's say a person is very upset and says something like:

> "You don't give a damn about me. You have this cushy job.. what a soft life, and you have some nerve telling me I can't [whatever the person wants to do]."

The customer is throwing bait at you. He accuses you of not caring, and being lazy, If you respond directly to these attacks, you are controlled by the other person, and playing the game by his rules.

You can respond indirectly, so the person knows you have heard, while sending the message that you aren't going to play this particular attack game.

> " When did you start thinking that we aren't concerned with your situation?"

The attacking person doesn't expect this ... you are confusing the attacker by not playing by the rules. If the attacking person responds to your question, you have now gained control of the interaction, since the person is now reacting to you rather than vice versa.

The general form of the WHEN questions is:

When did you start feeling (or thinking) that [rephrase a part of what the person said so that it is non-inflammatory].

If you are going to use this technique, or any technique that involves rephrasing of the client's remark, you must make sure that you rephrase in a non-inflammatory way. In other words, use Type 2 (cooperative) language and avoid repeating any hot words or phrases the client uses. Clearly you wouldn't rephrase the client's statement using the following words:

> "When did you start thinking that I don't give a damn about you, have a soft life, and have a lot of nerve?"

It sounds silly, but more to the point it focuses the attention of the customer on the very things you don't want to deal with. Take out all hot words and phrases when you rephrase.

Snapshot

Getting Control
You can regain some control of the interaction by using verbal self-defense techniques that cause the customer to have to stop and think. Then you use the gap to acknowledge the feelings.

.

Before we move on to the next self-defense tactic, one more point is important. For this tactic and the next one, you can't change the wording very much and expect it to work. For example, you can't replace the word when, with why. Saying "Why do you think we aren't concerned about your situation?", causes a very different reaction. For this reason, don't change the wording of the when question.

TACTIC 25: GOING TO COMPUTER MODE

Computer mode is another means of responding in a way that shows you are listening, but doesn't result in your taking the bait. It is also unexpected by the attacker so it tends to disrupt the attack chain.

Using the previous example:

> "You don't give a damn about me. You have this cushy job .. what a soft life, and you have some nerve telling me I can't [whatever the person wants to do]."

You can respond as follows:

That's interesting. Some people do think that there are people who have easy jobs.

Then you stop. Period. Dead stop. Don't explain. Don't defend.

Again, this response confuses people, since it is:

- ♦ unexpected
- ♦ neutral (neither a defense or counterattack)
- ♦ shows you aren't taking the bait

Because it is unexpected and confusing, it is likely to force the attacking person to stop and think.

The general form for Computer Mode is:

That's interesting (or some other neutral statement). Some people do think [feel] that [rephrase the attack in a bland neutral way].

TACTIC 26: THE TOPIC GRAB

Like the "when question", and "computer mode", the TOPIC GRAB is used to get someone to stop long enough in their tirade to pay attention to what you have to say. It is designed to exert some control over the interaction. Based on the self-defense principle that suggests you use the momentum of the attacker for your own benefit, the TOPIC GRAB is unexpected and surprising to the hostile person.

The topic grab involves taking something that the individual has said during their tirade, commenting on it or asking a question about it. What makes this different from simply asking a question about the issue at hand, is that you choose a topic that is not directly related to the complaint, but has been brought up by the client. In addition, the more the client is interested in the topic, the more likely it is that he/she will hesitate or stop the tirade. The topic grab is a technique to temporarily distract the client, and return the conversation to a more calm condition.

Snapshot

High Risk
Not all unexpected responses are high risk, high gain. You can use other surprise tactics that are not as "high risk, high gain" as the one in the example. Humor is often unexpected, but carries a high risk.

The best way to illustrate the technique is to give an example:

Client: *"What the hell do you expect me to do now. Look, I got fired for no reason, and you don't give a damn.. and now I ask for MY money back from my pension, and you tell me that I can't have MY money ... what kind of idiot are you, anyway. I got a family to support, I have a house with a mortgage, and because of you my family is going to end up on the street. How am I supposed to feed my kids ... what are they gonna think ..."* [and on and on]

Employee:[very calmly and in a tone that shows interest] *"It must be frustrating, Mr. Smith. How old are the kids?"*

Client: [stops and stutters a bit] *"Ummm ... five and seven. Why do you ask?"* [note that the client has relinquished control by responding to YOU]

Employee:*"Well, I have kids around that age too, and it sure is tough sometimes, isn't it. I know how difficult it is to worry about them. Let me explain what you can do, so at least you will know your options."*

Client:*"Well, this stinks ... it just isn't fair."*

Employee:*"Some people think it IS unfair let me explain what you can do next, OK?"*

TACTIC 27: THE BROKEN (STUCK) RECORD TECHNIQUE

If a person is talking angrily and not paying attention to what you are trying to say, it is a waste of time to get into any complex explanations. One tactic that people find useful is called the Broken (or Stuck) Record technique. This involves repeating one or two short sentences until the angry person starts to hear you.

What you choose to repeat is important. Choose language that shows that you are willing to help, and that you are concerned, rather than formal, bureaucratic language. For example:

Client: [talks on and on]

Employee:	*"Mr. Smith, it is frustrating Let me explain what you can do"*
Client:	[keeps talking abusively]
Employee:	*"I know you're frustrated. Let me explain what you can do ."*
Client:	[keeps talking abusively]
Employee:	*"It's frustrating. Can I explain what you might do next?*
Client:	*"Damn right it's frustrating."*
Employee:	*"It is. What you might want to do next is ...."*

TACTIC 28: TELEPHONE SILENCE

The self defense techniques presented in this chapter can be used in person or on the phone. Let's look at a tactic that is specifically designed to cause a phone caller to stop talking and respond to you.

 Snapshot

The Topic Grab
The topic-grab involves taking something that the individual has said during their tirade, and commenting on it or asking a question. This is a technique to temporarily distract the client and return the conversation to a calmer condition.

Like any kind of conversation, telephone interactions have rules. One of those rules is that when one person is talking, the other person sends signals to the "talker", so she knows there's someone still at the other end, listening This is necessary because the parties can't see each other. The only way to know there is a person on the other end is if the other person makes some sort of noise, usually "yes", "uh huh", "I understand ", etc.

Consistent with our self defense principles, you do not want to follow this rule. The best way to get a person to stop talking on the phone is simply to say nothing at all. If you can avoid breathing into the phone, or if you can exclude any noise getting through from your end, that's even better. Eventually, the person on the other end will stop, and say something like "Hello, hello, are you there?", and pause for a moment. This gives you the opportunity to say something at the invitation of the caller.

Let's look at an example:

The customer is talking to the employee over the phone.

Customer: *"Why are you people so inefficient? I have called six times today, and each time I get told the same thing .. what's wrong with you ... if you worked for a real company, you'd have gone broke years ago, and I am sick and tired..."*

[Note that the customer appears to have no intention of stopping and allowing the employee to help]

> **Employee:** [Actually says nothing, making sure not to use words like "yes", or "uh huh".]
>
> **Customer:** *"Hello, hello, are you still there?"*
>
> **Employee:** *"Yes, and I know you are frustrated. I WILL help you if you give me your name."* [employee uses a louder than normal voice, but still sounds firm and calm].
>
> **Customer:** *"It's Mr. Jones."*
>
> **Employee:** *"Thank you, Mr. Jones. Now, if I understand, you are upset because you haven't received credit for the merchandise you returned, right? Can I ask you a few questions to get to the bottom of this?"*
>
> **Customer:** *"Yeah, OK."*

Let's analyze this interaction. The customer is complaining and ranting. If the employee tries to interrupt, the customer is probably going to continue. The employee just keeps quiet. Eventually, the customer asks if the employee is still there, providing an opportunity for the employee to reassert control.

The employee uses the opening to ACKNOWLEDGE the customer's feelings and situation. He uses an empathy response, and emphasizes that the customer WILL receive help.

Once the customer responds by giving his name, the employee has re-established control and enters the next components of the CARP system.

The employee uses a LISTENING response, and then uses a question to replace a statement, REFOCUSING the customer on the reason he called.

The customer again responds, and for all intents and purposes, the attack has been stopped. If we followed the rest of the conversation, we would see that the employee then moves to the problem-solving stage.

Tactic 29: Allow Venting

A variation of the previous tactic works both in person and on the phone. It also involves silence.

CAUTION!

Not All People Vent Well
Some people, if left to vent, will end up feeding into their own upset, and get more and more agitated. If silence and venting seem to be having an unintended effect, try other techniques.

Remember that most angry and hostile people want to feel that you are listening to them. If you constantly interrupt, the message you will send is that you aren't listening, even if you are. This results in the customer increasing the intensity of the attack.

We also know that sometimes, a person needs to let off a little steam, before they can "get down to business". Rather than going head to head with the customer, it makes sense to allow the customer some time to vent his or her frustration, and to get tired (squawked out, so to speak). When the person starts to wind down, use acknowledgment techniques to prove that you are paying attention, then refocus and problem-solve as the person calms down.

TACTIC 30: YOU'RE RIGHT

This self-defense technique is a very powerful one. When a hostile person is nasty to you, he expects you to fight back; to defend or counterattack. The last thing he expects is for you to agree with something he has said. If you can find something to agree with, the attacker will be caught off guard. Creating agreement makes it appear that you and the customer are on the same side.

However, when you choose something to agree with, be sure that you aren't giving ammunition. Be clear about what you are agreeing to. Look at the example below:

> **Customer:** "Why is it taking so long...are you people stupid or something or are you just lazy ... I can't believe it."
>
> **Employee:** [using loud, strong tone] *"You're right! It IS taking a long time. I know it's frustrating. Let me see if anything can be done to speed things up, OK?"*
>
> **Customer:** [sarcastically] *"Yeah, sure, right."*
>
> **Employee:** *"OK, would you like me to get your file to see what the delay is about? Why not take a seat, and I'll be back in less than two minutes."*
>
> **Customer:** *"Alright, but be quick about it."*
>
> **Employee:** "I'll be just a moment."

If we analyze this we see that the employee confuses the customer into silence by agreeing that it IS taking a long time. Note the wording. The employee **isn't agreeing that it is taking TOO long**, since this supplies additional ammunition, but is simply echoing the opinion expressed. It sounds like the employee is agreeing, although the truth is the employee hasn't agreed to much at all.

Saying "You're right" brought control back to the employee, who seizes the opportunity by acknowledging the frustration, and offering help in the form of a question.

The customer isn't calmed down, but has started to scale down the attack. Then the employee asks a helpful question, and makes a suggestion.

TACTIC 31: REFRAMING TO COMMON GOALS

In any situation where two people disagree and the conversation takes a turn for the worse, a shift of focus occurs in terms how they see each other, and their goals. For example, let's consider the case where a customer wants to return an item after the time period allowed for returns, and in a condition such that the item cannot be resold. The customer's goal? It's simple. She wants her money back so she can spend it on something else, or at another establishment. The company, however, has a goal of limiting losses.

> ### Snapshot
>
> **Common Goals Always Exist**
> In any situation there will always be some goals held in common, and some goals that conflict. The trick is to focus on what is common between the two parties. When both parties embrace common goals, anything is possible.

In a conversation that escalates into hostility, what happens is that each "side" believes the other's goal is unfair, or otherwise inappropriate. Worse, the perception is that there are two mutually exclusive goals, and that erodes trust.

The customer believes that the company is trying to take advantage of her, or develops some other negative goal regarding the intent of the company, and the employee. On the flip side, the employee may come to believe the customer is trying to pull a fast one.

Once these beliefs or perceptions are in place, it's almost impossible to find some way out of the argument, because trust is gone, and the two parties are, indeed, on different sides.

You'd think that this is a situation where the whole conversation is a lost cause, but thankfully that's not the case. The key is to alter the way the customer perceives the company's goals, or your goals as a representative of the company.

In order to understand this, you need to understand that at any time, and in any situation involving people, there are a number of goals operative at any one time. People don't act in the service of one single over-riding goal or purpose, even if they believe they are doing so. We're much more complicated than that. We act on multiple goals and desires, and many of these are unconscious or in a "place" in our heads we don't access.

In situations where trust breaks down as a result of perceived incompatible goals, the key is to find other goals in the situations that both parties share, focus attention on them, and work from THAT common ground.

Let's consider the return of merchandise example, which appears to have two incompatible goals. It's a safe bet that amongst the customer's goals are:

♦   Happiness with the purchase

- Getting a good deal
- Feeling like they are not being taken advantage of

These are pretty much universal. Who doesn't want these things?

What about the company? What about the customer service employee? Can we state goals that are important to the company/employee that are compatible with and/or shared with the customer?

We can. On the company side, here's a few. The company wants

- Customers and that specific customer to be happy with their purchase so they'll return.
- Customers to feel they are getting a good deal.
- Customers to trust the company to not take advantage of customers.

 Bet You Didn't Know

Reframing
Any circumstance can be looked at in many ways. Reframing involves shifting one's own perceptions, and those of the other person away from destructive ways of seeing a problem to a constructive way of seeing the problem.
Focusing on common goals is going to be constructive almost all the time, whereas focusing on the disagreements hinders solutions. It is NOT about spin. It's about choosing a constructive perception.

At this point you should be seeing that even though there is some disagreement about the details of what constitutes a best path to achieving the goals of the parties, there are common goals operating here.

Why then is the conversation deteriorating? Because the mutual and complementary goals have been forgotten, often due to the heightened emotions of the moment. The solution is to focus the customer on these commonalities, so that the customer can re-establish some sense of mutuality, and of being on the same side even though there is disagreement about the details.

Once you establish that, you create a foundation for resolution, and a way for the customer to lower the emotional intensity involved in the situation.

That brings us to the idea of reframing, and refocusing. Reframing refers to a process where you encourage the other person to see the situation differently and in a more positive light. This process isn't about conning someone, or manipulating someone to accept a lie. It's also not about trying to put a positive spin on the situation. It is about acknowledging there are other ways to look at things, and to acknowledging the truth — that there is common ground. There almost always is at some level.

How do you do it?

The easiest way to grasp this is to look at an example of how it works. Here's a dialogue that illustrates how its done.

> **Customer:** *So, what's so special about two weeks? It's the same merchandize as before, it's just that I couldn't make it to the store to return it within two weeks.*

Employee: *We have some limits we apply, and there are some good reasons for having limits. We also have signs posted so that everyone knows what they should do if they want to return items.*

Customer: *Well, I wasn't told beforehand.*

Employee: *It's possible that you didn't notice the signs by the registers but as you can see, they are there, and they are in all our stores.*

Customer: *I don't believe you. There were no such signs when I made my purchase.*

Employee: *Maybe I'm not explaining this very well. We'd like you, as our customer, to be happy and satisfied when you purchase something from us. I'm sure you'd agree that we should be concerned with your satisfaction, right?*

Customer: *Well, yes. Of course. If I am not satisfied, I don't come back.*

Employee: *Exactly. We lose your business. That's not what we want. But we have to be concerned with the satisfaction of all our customers, not just you. If we didn't show concern and look after the interests of all customers, we'd be out of business.*

Customer: *Well that's your problem*

Employee*: You are absolutely right. It is our problem, but here's the thing. If you bought something that had been sitting in someone's basement for a month or so, and the packaging had been opened, would you be happy when you got it home?*

Customer: *Well, no. I guess I wouldn't. When I buy something here, I expect it to be brand new.*

Employee: *Good. We're on the same wavelength then. We want you and every customer to be happy and satisfied, and if we let people return things outside of the return period, we're going to make some other customer unhappy. That's not something we want. And if you were the other customer, that's what you'd expect.*

Customer: *Well, I guess. I never thought of it that way.*

QUICK EXPLANATION

In this example, the employee reframes the situation for the customer. It's not about the customer getting what she wants this time. It's about helping the customer to understand that when the company protects other customers from buying "old" merchandize, the company is protecting her to.

The process places the customer and employee on the same side, by focusing on the customer's satisfaction, albeit in a slightly different way. So, the reframe involves switching the focus from this particular event to the idea that the company must apply its rules to protect everyone, where everyone includes the current customer.

Note that the employee didn't talk about "policy" or "rules are rules" or any of the oft used explanations that are completely company centered. She didn't argue with the customer, and didn't take any of the bait or get intimidated.

CHAPTER CONCLUSION

We have presented self-defense tactics that are designed to help you get control over the interaction and/or turn a destructive conversation into a constructive one.. By using unexpected phrases and tactics, you can confuse the customer just long enough to begin using the other parts of the CARP model.

Like all of the defusing techniques, these must be combined with others, and we have tried to show you what that might look like in the dialogues presented.

Chapter IX — Acknowledgment Tactics

In this chapter we discuss several techniques to acknowledge the feelings and situation of the angry or hostile customer.

INTRODUCTION

Up to this point we haven't described the most important acknowledgment tactics we have -- empathy statements and active listening. Both of these tactics are relatively easy to learn, although some people feel that the use of empathy makes them sound weak. This isn't true. Before we discuss this, and the details of using these tactics effectively, let's review relevant principles.

Snapshot

Up to this point we have not described the most important acknowledgment tactics available. They are empathy statements and active listening. Both of these tactics are relatively easy to learn. However, some people feel that the use of empathy makes them sound weak. This just isn't true.

REVIEW

1. Angry and hostile people want their problems solved. They also need to feel understood and heard, before they will begin to calm down.

2. Angry and hostile people are not ready to problem-solve.

3. Acknowledging a person's emotional state and situation is a strategy that can be applied through out the defusing hostility process, but MUST be done early in the interaction, and before problem-solving occurs, since a furious person is not ready to problem-solve.

4. While you want to acknowledge the feelings of the customer, you don't want to dwell on those feelings for an inordinate amount of time. That's why you follow acknowledgment tactics with efforts to refocus the customer back to the original issue.

5. As with any defusing tactics, you want to be sure not to provide ammunition to the customer.

TACTIC 32: EMPATHY STATEMENTS

Empathy statements PROVE to the person that you understand their emotional state, be it angry, frustrated, etc. Empathy statements are most effective when you demonstrate that you also understand WHY the individual is upset.

We need to be absolutely clear here that empathy statements do not involve AGREEING with the client, or condoning his or her abusive behaviour. Empathy statements just convey that you are interested and concerned, and that you understand. Nothing more, and nothing less.

Before we look at examples of empathy statements, let's examine the question: Does the use of empathy statements make us sound weaker? Some people, particularly men, believe that talking about feelings makes them sound less authoritative and less strong. My experience is that this isn't the case. Often, people who are uncomfortable with using empathy statements are uncomfortable because they aren't used to using them, or because they do not often receive them.

Empathy statements allow the employee to relate to the customer in a non-bureaucratic way, and in a way that recognizes that the customer is a unique human being — a person with unique reactions.

CAUTION!

Avoid!
General statements such as "I hear you", and "I understand" are not true empathy statements because they lack detail that **proves** understanding. They don't work. Also avoid empathy statements that sound too touch-feely or that belong in a therapist's office.

EXAMPLES

Let's look at a few empathy phrases. In the next section we will provide you with some guidelines to use to ensure that your empathy statements are effective.

- ◆ *I realize you've been waiting a long time.*
- ◆ *It must be frustrating. It sounds like you're pretty annoyed.*
- ◆ *I guess you feel like you're getting the run around.*
- ◆ *It must be pretty difficult to make ends meet.*
- ◆ *It must seem like these things take forever.*

Notice how simple these statements are. **Short, to the point, and uncluttered** with other details. Also, note that there is nothing that shows that the employee agrees with the customer, only that the employee understands the situation.

GUIDELINES

1. Empathy statements are usually short and to the point. They can be used on their own, or they may be coupled with refocus statements, or other tactics. For example:

    Customer: *"I'm fed up with how long it takes for you to make a decision ... It's been 3 months already ..."* etc.

    Employee: *"I realize it's been a long time. It must be frustrating."*

    Customer: *"Damn right it's frustrating."*

    Employee: *"It must be. Let's see what we can do to speed things up. I need some additional information. Can I ask you a few questions?"*

At first, the employee uses the empathy statements and **STOPS**, allowing the customer to **RE-SPOND**. When the customer responds, the employee agrees it must be frustrating.

When the customer is very angry, we suggest that you use empathy statements and stop. Allow the customer to respond. If the customer appears to be too angry to carry on a rational conversation, continue to use single empathy statements, using the **BROKEN RECORD TECHNIQUE** from the previous chapter.

When the customer is not too angry, empathy statements can be coupled with other approaches from the beginning. For example:

> **Customer:** *"I'm fed up with how long it takes for you to make a decision ... It's been three months already ..."* etc.

> **Employee:** *"I realize it's been a long time. It must be frustrating. Would you like me to explain why it's taking this long?"*

In this example, the employee realizes the customer is angry, but not so angry as to be irrational. He uses an empathy statement along with a question that shows a willingness to provide information. And, he offers the customer a choice.

2.   Empathy statements should not include the word BUT. Remember what it was like to bring home your school report card? Often a parent would say something like: "Gee, Mary you got an 'A' in Math, but that English mark has got to improve." What did you remember? The compliment or the negative comment? The negative comment, of course. It works the same for empathy. Don't say something like:

> *I realize you've been waiting a long time, but all these people were here before you.*

> **or**

> *I know this is upsetting but you have to follow the law.*

When you have two things to say, one positive and one negative, don't use the word "but". Separate the ideas into different sentences. For example:

> *I realize you've been waiting a long time.* [pause] *There are a number of other people who have been here quite a while.* [Note the rephrasing of the last sentence. It is less blunt, but the customer will know what you are saying.]

3.   Empathy statements must not restate the idiotically obvious. If a customer is in your office, throwing things and yelling at the top of his lungs, it is probably not a good idea to say:

> *"It seems like you are just a touch annoyed."*

Since the customer's behavior clearly indicates the client is furious, not a touch annoyed, this statement is both inaccurate, and sounds patronizing. Better to simply say:

"Look, I know you're upset."

4.   Empathy statements require the proper tone of voice. You can make an empathy statement sound sarcastic, aggressive, or patronizing by the tone of voice you use. The best tone for empathy statements is a calm, matter of fact tone, so that it is clear to the receiver that you have no hidden agenda, and that you are making a simple statement of fact, rather than an accusation.

5.   Using "I" in an empathy statement has some risk attached to it. Remember you want to focus on the feelings of the other person, not yours. When you use I as a major part of your empathy statement, you run the risk of providing ammunition to the other person. For example:

> **Employee:**   *I understand how frustrating this is for you.*
>
> **Customer:**   *How could you possibly understand. YOU don't have to go through this ... etc*

Rather than beginning your empathy statement with "I", begin it with **"It seems like..."**

Then you are less likely to receive the kind of response shown in the last example.

TACTIC 33: LISTENING RESPONSES

 Snapshot

Empathy Tip
When the customer is very angry, we suggest that you use empathy statements and stop. Allow the customer to respond. If the customer appears to be too angry to carry on a rational conversation, then continue to use single empathy statements using the **Broken Record Technique** from the previous chapter.

Listening responses show that you are making the effort to listen to what the customer has to say, and that you are committed to getting it right. If you want to have a positive affect on another person you need to PROVE that you are listening.

Listening responses are useful for another purpose. Angry people are sometimes difficult to understand because the angrier they are the less coherent their speech. Sometimes it's difficult to get the details clear, or to understand what the real problem might be. Listening responses help you clarify the situation, so you don't end up in an argument due to misunderstanding.

Listening responses are again relatively simple. They involve rephrasing what the customer has said, and bouncing it back to the customer.

For example:

> **Customer:**   "Look, I completed this form before, and now you say I have to do it again! If you can't keep track of your paperwork, don't make me do your job ... blah blah."

Employee: "OK, let me make sure I understand. Are you saying that you already completed the form? If so, maybe I should check the file one more time."

The same principles that apply to empathy statements apply to listening responses, as do the principles of self-defense. When you rephrase what the client has said, **remove hot words, and harsh language.**

Below are two examples of how you can start off your listening responses:

"So, if I understand you correctly, you're saying that ... Is that correct?"

"I want to make sure I understand. Are you saying that..."

CHAPTER CONCLUSION

Acknowledgment tactics are surprisingly powerful considering how easy they are to learn. Of all the tactics in this book, the ones in this chapter are probably the most important.

With both empathy statements and listening responses, remember that it is necessary to prove to the other person that you are hearing and understanding. A cursory "Uh huh" or similar responses will not have a strong positive effect, while full fledged listening and empathy responses will.

This page left blank intentionally

Chapter X — Countering Non-verbal Intimidation

In this chapter we discuss non-verbal methods customers use to intimidate and control,, and what you can do about it.

INTRODUCTION

So far we've talked about the many ways that customers use language to gain control of the interaction, and put you off balance. That's not the whole story. Not only do people learn language in manipulative ways, but they also learn how to use nonverbal behavior to apply pressure, to make you nervous, and to convey negative messages to you.

No doubt you are familiar with these tactics. Think for a moment. Can you remember a situation where your customer was using nonverbal communication that made you feel uncomfortable?

In all likelihood, you are familiar with the following customer behaviors:

- invading your personal space
- staring you down (extended eye contact)
- using height to intimidate
- standing over you while you are sitting
- severe facial expressions
- pointing at you
- waving a finger in your face
- obscene gestures
- table pounding
- ripping up papers
- throwing things or knocking objects off table
- door slamming
- heavy sighs
- rolling eyes
- extreme fidgeting

It isn't pleasant to be on the receiving end of these tactics. Before we talk about ways you can counteract some of these behaviors, let's clarify a few points.

TAKING MEANING FROM NON-VERBAL BEHAVIOR

When I deliver a seminar, I usually ask about the kinds of nonverbal behavior customers use to intimidate. I usually get a list very similar to the one presented above. Occasionally I get a few suggestions regarding more subtle behavior, such as crossed arms or looking up to the left or some other direction. We need to be careful when we interpret nonverbal behavior that is in a gray ambiguous area. Is a person who has their arms crossed trying to intimidate? Or, is he cold? Or perhaps he's short on the "hug quota" for the day? It's hard to tell.

These days you can walk into a book store, and find books of the "how to read someone like a book" variety. You might read that head scratching means something, or looking up and to the right has a specific meaning. People have gone so far as to list dozens of these little behaviors, and interpret them for readers. If you believe these books, I have a bridge to sell you.

The truth is that nonverbal behavior can't be interpreted in such an exact way. Is the head scratcher suffering from fleas, or is he confused? The information you find in popular psychology books or new wave" psychology books is really more valuable to the authors than the readers. These books generate income for the authors, but their notions are so simplistic as to be useless and even dangerous.

The list of aggressive nonverbal behavior provided in the previous section is pretty reliable. While there are cultural differences (see below) that need to be taken into account regarding some of these actions, they are fairly reliable indicators of the customer's state of mind.

CULTURAL DIFFERENCES

The second point to be made is that different cultures have slightly different nonverbal patterns. Some groups are far more expressive, using gestures and tone of voice differently. People differ in terms of the length of time eye contact can be maintained, depending on their cultures and place of birth. Also, people differ in terms of the personal space (distance between you and them), they find comfortable.

 Bet You Didn't Know

Culture Doesn't Mean Just Ethnicity
Culture operates at many levels, and is not just related to ethnicity. For example there are geographical differences within the same country. There are differences due to socio-economic status, gender, and a multitude of other factors.
That's why it is almost impossible to made generalizations about this group or that group since every person in a group is also influenced by multiple "sub-cultures".

But here's the kicker. Within any cultural group, there are large differences among individuals. For example, there is a common stereotype that Native People (First Nations) prefer not to make eye contact for any period of time. However, if you spend time with First Nations people, you will find that the variation between people is huge. Some don't like eye contact that is held for a long time, but some don't give it a second thought.

You will find the same situation for other cultural groups. Perhaps the generalization applies to the person in front of you, but it is just as likely that it does not.

For this reason, we have to stress that you should make NO assumptions. Each person, regardless of background, has his or her own style. You must treat each customer as an individual, not as a Native person, or a Chinese person. By observing the individual, you will learn about them, and the meaning of their behavior. Applying generalizations and stereotypes will not help you understand the person in front of you.

COUNTERMEASURE STRATEGIES

We are going to focus on dealing with the three most common nonverbal techniques that customers use .

PROLONGED EYE CONTACT, INVASION OF YOUR PERSONAL SPACE, AND USE OF HEIGHT DIFFERENCES.

Let's imagine a situation where you and your customer are standing. The customer is angry and hostile, speaking in a loud voice, and moving closer to you. He stares at you while he talks. If he's taller than you, the closer he gets, the more you have to angle your head upwards to look at him. The closer he gets, and the higher up he is, the less likely you are going to feel comfortable and in control.

What do you do?

The most common, gut response is to step backwards. People tend to do this when they have been "triggered" by this kind of nonverbal behavior. They try to increase the distance between themselves and the other person by retreating a step or two.

CAUTION!

Physical Contact
In angry situations, once there is any physical contact, the chances of escalation into violence increases drastically.

Is this OK? Well, it's not dangerous, but think for a moment. If you move backwards what impression does it give the aggressor? Does it tell the person you are in control? Does it present a strong, firm, confident image? Is it likely to stop the person from entering your personal space?

The answer to all of these question is NO. When you move backwards, you present a weaker image to the customer. Since you are reacting to THEIR inappropriate behavior, you continue to allow him to control you. Most importantly, if someone is trying to dominate you by intruding into your personal space, he will simply move closer once again, causing you to move backwards.

Not a great way to exert control.

What else can you do? Well, you can hold your ground, or move forward, matching the person's intimidating tactics with those of your own. It's a stronger form of response.

There are real problems with this tactic. First, if you stand your ground, or move forward, **you are escalating the conflict**. You create a situation where physical contact can occur, and in these situations any physical conflict can quickly escalate to violence. So, if you move forward and bump the person, they may grab your arm, or shoulder. Then what? Whatever happens next is going to be destructive. Very, very bad.

Sometimes if you stand up to this kind of bullying, the other person will back down, but it's definitely a high risk, high gain maneuver. Don't do it. At least, if you back up, you are safer.

Snapshot

Backing Up

When you move backwards, you are presenting a weaker image to the customer. Since you are reacting to **their** inappropriate behavior, you are continuing to allow them to control you. And, most importantly, if someone is trying to dominate you by intruding on your personal space, they will simply move closer once again, causing you to move backwards.

If you can't back up, and you can't move forward, or hold your ground without risking a physical confrontation, what does that leave? Well, you could ask the person to step back. While this isn't a terrible response, it violates our rule of "What you focus on you get more of". By drawing attention to the issue, you let the person know he is succeeding in making you uncomfortable.

Here's the solution, the Stand Up Shuffle.

TACTIC 34: THE STAND UP SHUFFLE

The Stand Up Shuffle is based on something we know about nonverbal behavior. We know that when two people are angry they will tend to stand face-to-face and nose-to-nose. The nose-to-nose position is a confrontational position. However, there are two other positions that are perceived as less confrontational.

In the right angle position, each person is at right angles to each other. Take a look at Figure 1 on the following page. In example (a), the most confrontational position, the shoulders are parallel. In example (b), the shoulders are almost at right angles.

To reduce the sense of confrontation, and to feel more comfortable, you want to move from position (a), to position (b). You want to be at more of an angle to the intimidating person.

The third position (example c) is side by side. The side by side position is the most cooperative and is appropriate when two people are working cooperatively and when anger levels are lower.

So let's map this out. Imagine you are nose-to-nose. What you do is move your feet slightly (shuffle), so that your shoulders are no longer parallel. While you do this, you can also break eye contact with the individual. That helps to reduce the confrontational feel. The movement of your feet and shoulders actually increases the distance between you and the other person.

Now, you are slightly sideways to the person. Suppose the person wants to get in your face again. She has to follow you to get back into the confrontational position (a). Then, you simple respond by shifting back into your original position, so that you are again at an angle to the person. Most people will simply give up on this tactic if you do this properly. If you can imagine this in action, you will realize that it looks like a little dance.

But, who is leading the dance? You are. You are using very subtle non-verbal techniques to send the message that you will not be controlled.

One caution. You cannot turn so far so that the other person sees **any part** of your back. Do not turn to more than a 90 degree angle. This implies that you are dismissing the other person, and is inflammatory.

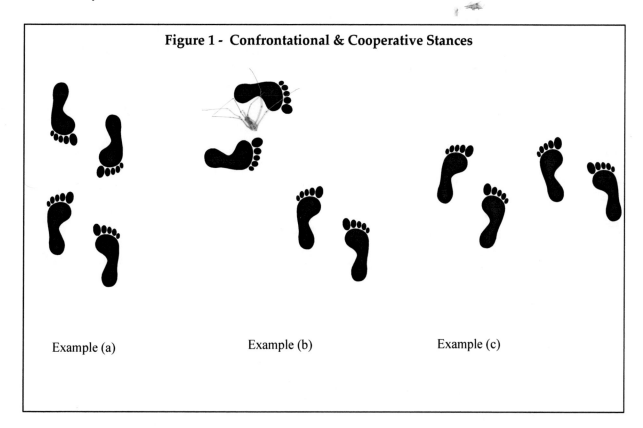

Figure 1 - Confrontational & Cooperative Stances

Example (a)   Example (b)   Example (c)

TACTIC 35: DISTRACTION

Another technique that works well, particularly when combined with the Stand-Up Shuffle, is distraction.

What we want to do is to provide a reasonable excuse to break eye contact, without appearing to be submissive, while at the same time, directing the person's eyes to something else. That something else could be a piece of paper (map, form, report, etc.), a computer screen, a piece of machinery, clipboard, or anything handy that may be relevant to the discussion. Let's see how it works:

A customer complains rather loudly that he is being charged extra because he asked for some substitutions on his pizza order. As the customer pays his bill he "gets in his face" of the cashier, obviously upset. The cashier turns somewhat sideways (stand-up shuffle) while at the same time, saying: *"Sir, let's take a look at the menu and see what's happened"* and holds out the menu so the customer can read it. The cashier continues (customer has broken eye contact to look at sheet and has stopped bellowing, since his attention switches to the menu.: *"If you notice, (pointing) you ordered the special, and just below it, it says that we charge for changes if customers want something different. We do that because it costs us more to customize our specials for you."* Meanwhile the cashier continues to focus attention on the menu.

While the customer is looking at the menu, he is unable to continue his intimidation tactics. If the location allows, the employee can move to the side-by-side position, to further defuse the situation.

The distraction technique works with people who are seated too. Get them to look at something else, and you will help break the tension that exists. Remember to point or otherwise physically direct their attention to a particular spot.

Let me give you another example:

An insurance adjustor is in the insurance company's garage. She has just explained how much the insurance company is willing to pay for the damage to the customer's car, but the customer is irate and complaining. The customer is taller than the adjustor, and moves closer, using nonverbal intimidation tactics.

 CAUTION!

Don't Show Your Back
One caution. You cannot turn so far so that the other person sees any part of your back. Do not turn to more than a 90 degree angle. This implies that you are dismissing the person and is inflammatory.

The adjustor takes control of the situation this way. She shuffles somewhat sideways, so she is facing the vehicle. Extending her hand to point to a lower portion of the car (around the wheel well), she says *"Take a look down there. Is there a dent there we might have missed?"* The customer naturally moves closer to the lower area of the car, and bends over to investigate, whereupon the adjustor moves slightly behind the customer. Because the customer is bending over, butt up in the air and head in the wheel well, he has lost his height advantage. At this point, the adjustor says: *"I could be wrong, Mr. Smith, but let's take one final look at the car, to make absolutely sure there is nothing we've missed."*

The adjustor has clearly taken control of the interaction, and sent a subtle message that she is not going to be intimidated. All without calling attention to the situation.

TACTIC 36: EQUALIZING HEIGHT

For those of you who interact with clients while sitting, be aware of the importance of equalizing height. If you are seated, and the other person is standing over you, you won't be able to feel confident or sound in control. The clear solution here is to stand up, or encourage the other person to be seated.

When you stand up, make sure you do so calmly and slowly. We recommend that you turn yourself to approximately right angles to the person. **Do not stand up and move into THEIR space.**

As you stand, you may want to suggest that the person take a seat. If she chooses not to, then continue the conversation from the standing position. You can also use a distraction tactic as you stand.

If the person does sit down at any point in the conversation, then it is appropriate for you to sit also.

CHAPTER CONCLUSION

When you deal with nonverbal hostility, be as subtle as possible. If you can shut it down without having to talk about it with the customer, that's a good thing. That's why the tactics in this chapter are so useful. Your customers will probably not even be aware of what you are doing to counter their aggression.

This page left blank intentionally

Chapter XI - Referral Techniques

Introduction

Referral techniques are tactics that involve another person or agency, separate from you and your client. While some tactics clearly fall into one of the four CARP categories, referral techniques can be classified in any of the categories. These tactics can help you control the interaction, acknowledge the customer's feelings and problem, and can help refocus the customer on the real issue. They can also help with the problem-solving process and provide the customer with help on subjects and topics where you can't offer assistance directly.

Referral techniques can be very effective. They are most appropriate when you realize that you will not be able to calm down or help the customer. This situation can occur when:

- you and the customer just can't get along
- you don't have the authority to make a decision on the issue
- the customer is complaining about something that has been decided at a much higher level in your organization
- you are getting triggered
- the customer has problems that can only be solved by someone or an agency outside of your company, or even a competitor.

In this chapter we will look at three referral tactics. The important thing to remember is that referral techniques must be used correctly. Poorly executed referrals make things worse and make it appear like you are dodging responsibility or "passing the buck".

Tactic 37: Referring to Supervisor

You have probably come across the following situation:

You are dealing with an angry customer who just won't calm down. As the conversation goes on, the person becomes more abusive and irate. At some point in the conversation the client demands to see your supervisor. You arrange this, and the customer and your boss meet. After about five minutes, the customer leaves. As the client leaves you he seems much calmer - almost content.

You are curious as to what magic words the supervisor used to have such a profound effect on the customer — to turn the person from a lion to a pussycat. So you ask. Your supervisor says: *"Well, I pretty much said exactly what you said"*.

And the truth is, that's likely what happened. You see, it's not just what is said, or how it's said, but also **who says it** that makes a difference.

We know that people tend to be more abusive and hostile to employees they perceive as having less status and power. We know that hostile customers tend to treat people they think have status and power with more respect and politeness than people they think are at the "bottom" of the organization.

There is another principle that applies. Customers perceive the first person they talk to about their purchase or product dissatisfaction as having less power and status than the next person they talk to.

In other words, if they first talk to a receptionist, are then referred to a trouble-shooter, they will see the trouble-shooter as "more important". Or, if they first talk to a trouble-shooter, they will perceive the trouble-shooter's supervisor as "more important" when they are referred to see that person.

This suggests that referring to a supervisor may be a way of capitalizing on this phenomenon. If an angry, abusive customer will automatically treat a supervisor with more respect and be more reasonable, doesn't it make sense to offer this option to the individual? Yes. Experience of countless customer service representatives tells us that a good deal of time can be saved by offering this option to the customer early on in interactions that appear to be going nowhere.

There is another reason why "referring" is important. You may not have the authority to change a company rule, but your supervisor or manager may have that authority. In this situation, it makes sense, after trying to defuse the individual, to pass him on to the person who **CAN** help them. Just the act of offering to refer gives the impression that you are making the effort to help. That in itself can help to calm down the individual.

But, remember one thing. The referral technique is far more powerful if **YOU** offer it, rather than waiting until the customer demands it. By offering it, you show you are taking the initiative to help, and you are taking control of the interaction. If you wait until the customer demands it, you create the appearance that the customer is in control.

DOING IT RIGHT

Referring to a supervisor is a process that can be done well, or done poorly. Keep in mind that referring will be most successful when:

- ♦ it is offered by the employee
- ♦ the offer includes choices for the customer
- ♦ the supervisor is able to take control of the situation immediately
- ♦ it appears to the customer that you and the supervisor have taken the time to discuss the situation with each other
- ♦ the supervisor appears informed about the situation

Let's look at the steps in the referral process:

1. Determine you aren't getting anywhere.
2. Ask/offer if customer would like to speak with supervisor.
3. Notify supervisor of situation (out of earshot of customer) and explain to supervisor in private: customer's emotional state, situation's problems and relevant facts, what the customer has said, what you have said.
4. Supervisor greets customer.
5. Supervisor explains his or her understanding of situation to client.
6. Supervisor uses **CARP** techniques

Let's look at each of these in turn:

Determine you aren't getting anywhere. If the customer is getting angrier and angrier, even though you have used other defusing techniques, it's time to cut your involvement short, and refer. Or, if it is clear you don't have the authority to help, a referral is indicated.

Ask/offer if customer would like to speak to supervisor. Here are some phrases you can use:

> *"Sir, I don't think I can help you, but my supervisor is available. Would you like to speak to her?"*

> *"Mrs. Jones, I'm not able to approve what you want, so to save time, how 'bout if you talk to my supervisor? Would you prefer to wait, or would you like me to ask her to call you?"*

Note that we are offering the customer the choice, and we are careful not to over-commit the supervisor. We wouldn't say something like *"My supervisor will give you what you want"*, because that may not be the case and builds false expectations.

After the customer has consented, explain you will return in a moment.

Explain to supervisor. Approach the supervisor (see Tactic 38 for information about getting on the same wavelength), and explain the situation. For example:

> *"Got a problem. Mrs. Jones wants to [..] and I have told her that we can't legally do that. I have also said that [..] and she has been yelling and disrupting the office. Can you see her?"*

Presumably the supervisor will consent.

Supervisor makes contact. When you and the supervisor return to the client, we want the supervisor to grab and maintain control of the situation from the beginning. For this reason, the supervisor

 Bet You Didn't Know

Status and Abuse
We know a few things about angry behavior: Angry people tend to be more abusive & hostile to employees they perceive as having less status & power. Angry people tend to treat others they think have status and power with more respect & politeness than those they perceive to be at the "bottom"of the organization.

should introduce him/herself, rather than you making the introductions. While it may be more "polite" for you to introduce the supervisor and then back off, it is more powerful if the supervisor can approach the customer, and before he/she has had an opportunity to restart the complaint, the supervisor says:

> *"Hello, Mrs. Jones. I'm Ingrid, supervisor of operations. I understand that you want to [...] and that you are upset that it isn't possible. Is that correct?"*

We hope the customer replies *"yes"*. At that point the supervisor can invite the customer into further discussion. For example:

> *"OK, why don't we go into my office so we can discuss this and see what the situation is?"*

<u>What we want to avoid at all costs is forcing the client to explain his/her situation over again.</u> First, it aggravates the customer, but more importantly, it allows the customer to take control.

CAUTION!

Don't Make Customer Repeat
If you force the customer to repeat the whole problem to the supervisor, you waste a valuable opportunity, and will further anger the customer.

So, it is NOT effective for the supervisor to say: *"What seems to be the problem, here?"* This will just restart the complaint.

That's the basic tactic. But there is a bit more to this. Obviously, you and your supervisor need to be on the same wavelength for this to work. This is **SO** important that we have included a separate tactic to help you create a situation where the above technique will work.

TACTIC 38: PLANNING FOR REFERRAL

It should be clear to you that you and your supervisor need to be on the same wavelength about referrals. Your supervisor may not want to be involved in some situations, but may want to be involved in others. You and your supervisor need to agree on how these situations will be handled. For this reason, I recommend that you approach your supervisor to discuss some of the questions listed below. And, if you are a supervisor, I suggest you talk to your staff about those same questions. Supervisor and employee need to be clear about when and how referrals can be carried out.

- ♦ Under what conditions does the supervisor want to be involved?
- ♦ How often can you refer to the supervisor?
- ♦ What does the supervisor want to know about the customer beforehand?
- ♦ When will the supervisor be available for referrals?
- ♦ Does the supervisor have any preferences about the mechanics of the referral?

This information must be shared between supervisor and employee in advance. I recommend that the subject be revisited at least once a year.

When we discuss the next two referral tactics, you will discover that planning is equally important to the success of those techniques, too

TACTIC 39: REFERRING TO CO-WORKER

Some employees interacting with clients or customers on a daily basis have told me their supervisors are unwilling to be involved with angry customers. Occasionally, I hear this: *"Whenever there's a problem, it seems my supervisor has the amazing capacity to become invisible ... nobody can find him/her."* Well, it happens. We can grouse about it, or we can see what other possibilities are available.

Referring to a co-worker capitalizes on the same principles regarding status and power as referring to the supervisor. Co-worker referrals can be used when a supervisor is unavailable, or as a step prior to referring to supervisor.

Specifically, you can refer a customer to a colleague at the same level in the organization as yourself. You do this in almost the exact same way you would refer to the supervisor, using the same steps. The one difference is in your phrasing. What you want to do is to phrase things in a way that enhances the status and ability of the "third party in". Look at the following example:

You are dealing with a hostile customer who is getting increasingly agitated. You recognize that you just aren't getting through but you think that your colleague, Mary Ann, may have better success, and that a fresh approach might work. You say:

"Sir, you know, I don't think I can help you with this, but we have an expert on staff that deals with your situation quite often. Would you like to speak to MaryAnn?"

Take a look at what has been done. We are presenting Mary Ann as more experienced — an expert. This builds up their status in the organization without lying or over-committing Mary Ann.

You will find that in this situation, the customer may assume that Mary Ann is at a higher level in the organization. This is fine, since you haven't lied about her position, only called her an expert. And, if the customer sees Mary Ann as having higher status in the organization, he/she is likely to treat her with more respect. This means less time wasted, and less argument.

Remember you and your colleagues must be on the same wavelength about doing this. So, make sure you apply Tactic 38 — planning beforehand, so each player knows what to do. And, follow the principles and process described in Tactic 37, 'Referring to Supervisor'.

TACTIC 40: DIRECTING PERSON'S ANGER

There are times when a customer is angry at a situation not under your control, or even under the control of anyone in your immediate organization. Regulations, policies, even store layouts are

CAUTION!

Honesty Counts
When referring to a co-worker, it's ok to tell the customer that he or she has special skills or knowledge, but don't outright lie. Lying almost always backfires. Be conservative in your praise.

often determined at "head office" levels by people you've never met - executives or managers. This doesn't stop a hostile customer from complaining to you about these rules or regulations even though you have no authority to change the them.

In these situations, it is not effective to say "Sir, *that's not my job to make those decision*", or "Don't *yell at me, it isn't my fault.* " Both of these are defensive and come across as bureaucratic and certainly unhelpful.

What you may be able to do is direct the person's anger to a person or agency that has some responsibility for the policy/rule/regulation. Take a look at this example:

> **Customer:** *"Who the hell makes up these stupid policies? What a bunch of idiots ... You guys around here don't have a clue about what it's like to run a business...."*

> **Employee:** *"Sir, I know you disagree with the policy. If you want to have your say about this, the best thing to do is to contact* [head office, person, policy]. *They are involved in setting the policies. Would you like me to write down a name and phone number for you?"*

There are several things to notice in the example. First, notice the employee combines several techniques

Initially, she acknowledges the customer's concern. Then she provides information, and makes a helpful suggestion in a non-defensive tone. Then she offers a choice to the customer.

Several things to consider. First, most people will **NOT** take the time to follow-up. That takes effort, and often by the time the person gets home, he has calmed down enough to say *"Nah, I won't bother"*. Directing the person's anger weeds out people who are just complaining to get to you, and those that are serious about their complaint.

Second, directing the person's anger may be annoying to the person who ends up having to listen to it. Some managers and executives feel that the less contact they have with problems the better, and may not appreciate your efforts. If you direct the person's anger to the wrong person, or to someone who is unwilling to deal with the person, you create more problems. So be careful.

Again, the notion of being on the same wavelength is important. All employees in the same location should know to whom they can refer angry customers. Perhaps the Chief of operations hates this stuff. Well, you want to know. However, maybe there's an employee who reports directly to the chief that is receptive. Or, vice versa. These things need to be discussed with management so that you know what is OK and what is not OK.

TACTIC 41: REFERRING TO AN OUTSIDE SOURCE OR COMPETITOR

There are many situations when a customer has a need or want that you cannot accommodate. Sometimes the customer is angry, and sometimes frustrated that you cannot do what has been asked. A company can win huge public relations points by referring customers to those that can help, even if the ultimate destination takes the customer elsewhere, or even to a competitor. The reasoning is that they will still return to you because you were the person that initiated the process to solve the problem.

Snapshot

Referring To Outside Source
There are many situations when a customer has a need or want that you cannot accommodate. Sometimes the customer is angry, and sometimes frustrated that you cannot do what has been asked. A company can win huge public relations points by referring customers to those that can help, even if the ultimate destination takes the customer elsewhere, or even to a competitor.

Take the example of a hotel that has lost a customer's reservation and is fully booked. The customer arrives, and is understandably upset. It happens. The well trained hotel staff refers the customer to a competitor's hotel, AND follows the rules of referral by calling around to find a place for the guest and making arrangements to have the room held for the customer.

While that's not a perfect solution, it provides help to the customer, eases the interactions, and hopefully reduces hostility. Will the customer come back to the hotel that messed up the reservation? Maybe. Maybe not. We do know that if the hotel staff doesn't try to help by referring, there is no way the customer is returning.

This also applies when there has been no mistake but the customer is simply at the wrong establishment. Take, for example, a law office that deals only in corporate law. A distraught person calls about being sued by a neighbour who slipped and fell on the sidewalk in front of the caller's home. Only, the law office doesn't deal with those kinds of cases. What is the correct course of action? The employee can explain it's outside the purview of the office, and end the conversation. Or, he can provide a few alternate companies, along with names and phone numbers, so the customer (in this case the potential customer) can get in touch with someone who CAN help.

The employee can go even further, by making the call to an appropriate law office, and then connecting them via a conference system. Connecting a customer with someone who can solve their problem is a good thing.

Here are some similar situations where referral outside to company is appropriate.

♦ Customer arrives at restaurant hoping to order a particular kind of food that the restaurant doesn't serve. Solution? Refer them to an establishment down the street that does serve the dishes. Next time the customer is looking for what the restaurant can provide, guess where they will go. Straight to you.

♦ Electronics retailer has run out of stock on an item the customer wants badly (and quickly). They have no idea when or if that item will be available. The employee can try to sell something different, or perhaps provide a rain check on the basis that the item will eventually be available. Neither of those results in a happy customers. Refer them to a competitor and you establish yourself as an amazing store willing to lose a sale to make the customer happy.

♦ A car owner comes in to an auto body shop needing some repairs. She's travelling and is in a hurry, but the auto body shop is overbooked and can't do the job. Put the customer off? No way. Get on the phone and call competitors in the area to see if anyone else can do the job. There's no real loss here, since the first shop isn't going to close this deal anyway. Or provide names, addresses and phone numbers to the customer so she can contact them herself.

Tips and Suggestions To Make This Work

♦ As an employee, you need to make sure it's ok with your manager/boss to send a customer to another establishment. It's best to ask before you are in the actual situation so you will not delay the customer further by having to get permission.

♦ If you are a business owner or manager, establish guidelines for employees on when it's appropriate to send customers elsewhere and make sure your employees understand them.

♦ Have a list of other resources to provide for customers in the event that you can't accommodate them. Do your best to include a contact person, phone number, website, or any other information that might be useful in helping a customer contact or get to the other business.

♦ It's always a good step to undertake contacting the other business on behalf of the customer to find out if they can help, and to explain and introduce the customer. For example, get a person's name so the customer can ask to speak directly to that person when he or she arrives at the business, so the person doesn't have to explain the situation again.

CHAPTER CONCLUSION

Referral techniques can be very powerful ways of defusing hostile customers. When you refer properly, you appear helpful and concerned, particularly if you offer the option before the customer demands it. And, of course referrals capitalize on the status issue. We can use it rather than let it use us.

Finally, let's talk about one other point. It is often frustrating to have one's decision reversed by a supervisor or someone higher up. When you are diligently applying appropriate policies and regulations, and an executive, in effect, makes an exception or breaks that regulation, it can be upsetting. Keep in mind that the reversal usually has nothing to do with you personally. It doesn't mean you are incorrect, only that the person reversing your decision has a perspective that differs from yours. It's not uncommon for someone with more clout than you have to give in to a customer's demands simply to "get rid of the customer."

It happens all the time. You probably aren't going to change it, and it goes with the job. If you get all bent out of shape about this reality of making exceptions to the existing rules, you are only going to harm yourself.

This page left blank intentionally

Chapter XII — Time Out! Disengaging

Introduction

We have only one tactic to be discussed in this chapter. If you have had any formal training in parenting, or teaching, you have probably come across the notion of the time-out. A time-out is used when children are out of control, and exhibiting inappropriate behavior. The technique is also used with adults in some situations and "fits" where the individual is too emotional to conduct a constructive conversation.

The idea behind the time-out is not to punish the individual acting inappropriately, but to provide some time for reflection, so the person can regain self-control. A second purpose of the time-out is to remove the child from his/her peers, who may be involved in keeping the inappropriate behavior going (audience effect). Finally, the time-out, at least for children, is designed to teach them that there are consequences to their actions, and that they will be held responsible for their own behavior.

Snapshot

Disengaging
Disengaging involves creating a period of time when the interaction is "put on hold" to allow the person some time to think about what he/she has been saying, and an opportunity to save face. It differs from time-outs with children in terms of the way you communicate, since you are working with an adult.

While time-outs may be appropriate for children, their effectiveness is based on the ability of the person who IMPOSES it to enforce it. You are not in such a position with your customers. You can't say to an adult: *"I'm going to put you in a room by yourself until you calm down. When you are ready to behave you may come out."* At least, you can't say that to an adult and expect any positive outcome. It's patronizing and offensive.

What you can do is use a process called disengaging. The idea behind disengaging is to allow the person some time to think about what he/she has been saying, and to provide an opportunity to save face.

TACTIC 42: DISENGAGING

We know that a person acting in a hostile, abusive manner is unlikely to stop in the middle of his tirade and apologize. Even if he realizes he's acting unfairly, or is flat-out wrong, it's hard for anyone to make a sudden about face and apologize. It is simply too embarrassing.

However, a person who realizes he is wrong may apologize if there is a "break in the action". For some reason, when there is a break, there is a psychological sense that the conversation is starting anew. And since it is starting anew, the customer is more likely to back down or apologize without feeling he has lost face.

As with time outs for children, disengaging allows the individual some time for reflection. As we have mentioned before, angry people act quickly and without great thought. Force them to think, or provide an opportunity for them to think and often they conclude they are going about things the wrong way.

CAUTION!

Customer In A Hurry?
If and when a customer expresses concern about time passing, or being in a hurry, any process that seems to slow things down will, more than likely, inflame the customer.

Disengaging, or taking a break in the conversation can be effective in getting control over the interaction, and allowing the customer to think and act differently.

One more reason you may want to disengage is to allow **YOURSELF** some time to reflect and get your own feelings under control. If you find that a person is "getting to you", it may be best if you disengage for a moment, take a few deep breaths, and then return.

While disengaging means calling a temporary halt to the conversation, it doesn't mean walking away without a word, or walking away in a huff. You must present a plausible reason for removing yourself from the presence of the hostile customer. You take a brief break, and return again to take control of the interaction.

Take a look at the following example:

> **Customer:** *"Every time your mechanics change the oil in my car you find huge problems with my vehicle to get me to spend more money. I just think you have it in for me, and I can't stand dealing with you, you F*** * * A *** * **."* [customer continues despite efforts by employee]

The mechanic realizes that to continue at this time would be pointless. The customer is not ready for rational discussion.

> **Mechanic:** *"You know, Mr. Talbot, I know you dislike bringing your car in and always getting bad news. I have something I want to show you that might help, but it's in the back office. Can you just hold on a moment while I get it?"*

[Mechanic goes to the back office and retrieves an article that briefly discusses how a car owner was sued and lost his home due to a safety issue with a vehicle neglected to fix — a brake problem, that caused an accident. He returns to the customer service area, holding out the article to the car owner and says].

> **Mechanic:** *"Here, Mr. Talbot. I don't want to alarm you, but you may want to read this so you understand why it's so important that we find any safety issues that might put you at risk, so something like this won't happen to you* [this is also a distraction technique to focus attention from the customer's anger].]

> **Customer:** [quickly glances at but does not read article] *"I know why! Look, I know you are just trying to do your job, but it's always bad news. You guys cost me a lot of money.*

Mechanic: *"I realize that you understand why we tell you about car problems we might find. I know it's a hassle for you, but let's see how it works out. After all, the last time we serviced the car,, the only concerns were small ones, right?"*

Customer: *"Ya, I guess".*

Here is a situation where the owner expresses suspicion about the various repairs the garage discovers during regular maintenance.. He is so upset, the mechanic realizes nothing can be done through discussion <u>at that point</u>. Rather than go right into the tornado of emotion, the mechanic disengages, retrieves something to show the customer, and returns. You will notice that he also acknowledges the vehicle owner's dislike of mechanical inspections.

When he returns, he doesn't wait for the customer to speak, but immediately seizes the conversation. He brings something to use to distract the customer. In this situation, the short break in the conversation allows the customer to realize he is being unreasonable. His tone has changed from very aggressive to more of a pleading for understanding. At this point the inspector knows that the storm is over.

PLAUSIBLE REASONS

There is almost always something you can find that will sound like a plausible reason for disengagement. You can:

- ♦   consult a colleague
- ♦   consult your supervisor
- ♦   check policy or laws
- ♦   check a file or computer screen
- ♦   offer to get a cup of coffee for the client

VARIATIONS

Consider offering choices to the customer when you disengage. For example:

"Sir, I want to check the policy just to make sure I have it right. I'll just be a minute".

"If you like you can wait here, or take a seat in my office, whatever would be more comfortable. What would you prefer?"

CONCLUDING POINTS

When you disengage, it should be for a short time only. Use your best judgment, because a long disengagement is more likely to anger your customer rather than calm him or her down.

When possible arrange for the customer to be alone during the disengagement, or at least in a situation where it will be difficult to talk to someone. If he has other people he can talk to during the "break", he is less likely to reflect on his own hostile behavior and more likely to be egged on by bystanders or bother other customers in an attempt to get "support".

Some organizations have built small rooms for this purpose. The disengaged customer can be brought to this room, where she has little else to do but think. Left on her own for two minutes, experience indicates that she is likely to calm down provided the process is well executed.

Chapter XIII — Problem Solving

INTRODUCTION

The final component of the CARP system is problem solving. While we can talk about the importance of control and acknowledgment, when all is said and done, the customer hopes and expects that we will do something to help her with her problem or issue.

But, often we can't do exactly what the customer wants. Perhaps the customer has expectations that are totally unrealistic and based on a limited understanding of laws, regulations or business practices. Just as often, the customer will have only a vague idea of what she wants you to do.

The importance of problem solving lies in showing the customer that you take the complaint seriously, demonstrating you are making the effort to do SOMETHING, even if that something is not exactly what the client wants. Often, doing SOMETHING can be quite helpful, and that something often involves problem solving with the client.

WHAT IS PROBLEM SOLVING?

Problem solving involves a dialogue between you and the other person with the following goals:

- to arrive at a decision regarding what YOU will do, taking into account the rules and regulations and constraints you work under AND the concerns of the client.

- to determine courses of action that the CLIENT can take to pursue his/her own needs and concerns, taking into account the rules and regulations of the system.

Notice what is important is that both of these goals take into account two things the <u>realities of the organization's rules and regulations</u>, and the <u>needs and concerns of the client.</u> Both must be present to problem solve in a way that will calm down a hostile client. The solution has to work for BOTH sides.

Problem solving is a complex area, and there are literally, hundreds of problem solving models out there. It might be worth a search on the Internet to examine a few on your own to identify what approach "speaks" to you, since the model needs to fit with how you work and think.

Take note though. Most problem solving models are based on the assumption that problem-solving is a logical process, and in some ways it is. However, all human problem solving is affected by emotional states, agendas on both sides that may be conscious/known or unconscious/unknown and unstated.

Real world problem solving done with two or more people is subject to these factors, making problem solving both a logical process and one that involves working with hidden assumptions, emotions, and often, plain old stubbornness.

While we don't have space to present various problem solving models here, we can provide an overview for you. If you need more information, we suggest that you look for books and other resources available on the subject. However, briefly here are the steps:

1. Define the customer's concerns or problem
2. State your own requirements and limitations (Share Information)
3. Explore alternatives available
4. Work to agreement on course of action
5. Follow-thru

Even such a simple set of steps isn't always executed in sequence. You may think you've done the first two steps well, and believe there is mutual understanding of where you have been, but you might then discover that there isn't mutual understanding at all. In those situations you have to go back to previous steps, revise to accommodate any new information that comes up from the interaction, and go through it all again.

That's par for the course. It's normal, so expect it in any problem solving situations involving other people. There's a lot of **test-try-restart-retest** in the process.

TACTIC 43: DEFINE CUSTOMER'S CONCERNS & PROBLEM

 Snapshot

Expect Some Frustration
While problem solving may seem like a logical process, when two people work together, they start acting like human beings, sometimes acting irrationally and stubbornly, sometimes even resisting solving the problem. It's normal to have to go through the problem solving steps a few times to re-clarify.

Your first step is to strip away the superficial concerns presented by the client and find out what is REALLY the problem. This is often called <u>identifying the root cause.</u>

You can't help a customer unless you know exactly what the customer's problem is. Often the customer expresses vague concerns or shows unfocused anger. Your first step is to work to "get beneath" the superficial concerns presented by the client and determine the client's real concern. Let's take a concrete example. A customer contacts you regarding a charge on his telecom/internet bill that he feels he didn't consent to and doesn't want to pay. He feels that the charge is unwarranted and calls you to complain.

Customer: *Look, I sure as hell didn't download a terabyte of data, I can tell you that. Obviously something is wrong at your end. The numbers you claim are insane, and I'm not paying $80 in overuse fees. My wife saw the bill and hit the roof, and she's blaming me.*

[Note: What is the customer's problem here? It SEEMS clear but is it? We could take his complaints at face value, but maybe there's more to the story.

Employee: *So, you're concerned that there was a mistake made?*

Customer: *Of course I am. How the heck am I supposed to explain this to my wife? She thinks I've been downloading porn all month.*

Employee: *I can understand why that's a concern. So, there's two parts to this? There's the chance it's an error, and you are concerned that people will think you've been doing something wrong on the Internet, right?*

Customer: *Damn right. The money is bad enough but I have to deal with a very upset wife.*

[Now we've gotten to the core of the problem, and the employee can now try to address both issues for the customer. Addressing only one of the two issues won't work.]

Employee: *OK, I'm going to take a look at your usage log to see what's happened. Ok. I have it in front of me. Ah. I see something. Are you a baseball fan?*

Customer: *Yes, avid baseball fan. Why are you asking.*

Employee: *Here's what I'm seeing. I bet you've signed up for Major League Baseball games over the Internet offered by MLB, because I'm seeing a lot of connections to them.*

Customer: *Well, yes, I started in April, and I watch a game or two every day.*

Employee: *You probably didn't realize this but each game you watch takes about twenty gigabytes to view. If you are watching that many games, that accounts for the over use.*

Customer: *No, I didn't' know that. I thought it was all included in what I pay MLB.*

Employee: [Explains a course of action] *Sir, I have some solutions to both of your problems. First, we should look at the package you have with us, and see if you can save money by paying a bit more each month, but you'd not have to pay overuse fees again. For the other problem, I can arrange to send you a log of your usage, so you can explain to your wife that it's because of the baseball, and not from doing things she disapproves of. Does that work for you?*

Or, I can talk to her and explain if she's available.

Customer: *Yes, please.*

ANALYSIS:

Snapshot

Importance of Problem Solving
The importance of problem solving is that it shows the customer you are taking their complaint seriously, and making the effort to do SOMETHING, even if that something is not exactly what the client wants. Often, doing SOMETHING can be quite helpful, and that something often involves problem solving with the client.

What you see here is an employee making the effort to find out what the customer's problem is, and then moving to the problem-solving process. By using this approach, the employee is making an honest effort to understand, and help. Make special note of how the employee works to define the problem by asking questions, and using reflective listening responses to get the customer to go deeper into the issue.

Another important thing to remember is that if the client had been absolutely furious, this approach would not have worked. To problem-solve, the client must be calm enough to think clearly, to focus on the problem, and to listen. If the client is not yet to this point, then you have to use the Control, Acknowledgment and Refocus strategies FIRST. You can't problem solve until the person is acting reasonably.

TACTIC 44: PROVIDE INFORMATION

Customers don't necessarily understand the system they are involved in — they have odd notions of your role, and the role of your employer. In problem solving it is critical that you explain the reasoning behind the way things are done, AND, your own limitations. The customer needs to know:

♦ What you can and can't do
♦ Why you can't do what is desired
♦ How it might benefit them for you to follow the rules and procedures, when and if it's possible to explain those benefits.

An important part of the problem solving process is to put your cards on the table. You see this in the previous example. While it's not included in the dialogue on the previous page, the employee probably would have also explained why there's a usage cap, and how having one protects everyone, even the caller. This demonstrates he is making an effort to explain, and that's important.

Some phrases may be useful to help you provide information.

♦ *Sir, let me explain what I can and can't do for you.*
♦ *Were you aware that our job is to make sure everyone is protected?*
♦ *Perhaps nobody has taken the time to explain the situation to you. That could be our fault. Let me try.*

Tactic 45: Offer Alternatives & Suggestions

The customer WANTS you to be helpful, and one way to appear helpful is to take the time to make suggestions regarding what the person can do next — the CHOICES available. Remember we mentioned earlier that clients often feel helpless when interacting with bureaucracy and rules, and this sense of helplessness fuels their anger and hostile behavior. By offering suggestions and alternatives, we tell the customer he does have options to address some or all of his concerns.

Snapshot

Do What You Promise and Don't Over Commit
When you reach some agreement on a course of action, make sure that you can follow thru. You MUST do what you offer to do, so don't make promises you can't keep. Keep in mind that promises involving other people are harder to keep than promises you make that you alone will keep.

Offering alternatives/suggestions can also involve suggestions about what YOU can do, in addition to what the client can do. When offering choices that involve a number of steps, and where it is possible, write down the steps for the customer in sufficient detail so the information makes it easier for the customer to resolve the issue.

Tactic 46: Follow-Thru

When you reach some agreement on a course of action, make sure that you can follow-thru. You MUST do what you offer to do, so this means that you don't make promises you can't keep. Keep in mind that promises involving other people are harder to keep than promises that only involve you. For example, in some situations you may not be able to promise that "John will call you back in the next five minutes", since John might not be available. What you can say is:

"I'll talk to John, and either John or I will get back to you in five minutes."

If you make a promise you can't keep, even if it involves another staff member, YOU are still responsible for contacting the customer to let her know. For example, if you go to speak to John, and discover he is not able to discuss the customer's problem at that time, you STILL need to contact the customer within five minutes, since that's what you promised. So you would follow-thru by saying:

"Mr. Jones, I couldn't talk to John about your problem, but didn't want you to think I had forgotten about you. Here's what I suggest." [offer alternative suggestion].

Some Support Tactics

Before we end the chapter, let's talk about a few other tactics that you can use during problem solving.

Tactic 47: Create Agreement

Expert negotiators and mediators know that getting two people to agree to anything will open the door to agreement on the real issues, so, they start by creating agreement on little things first. You can use this technique in your own work. If the client says something you CAN agree with, make it clear that you DO agree (recall the use of agreement as a self-defense technique?).

Create agreement by asking questions that are almost guaranteed to get agreement. For example:

> *"I'm sure that you want to settle this as quickly as possible, right?"*

How many people are going to disagree? Not many.

Or CREATE agreement as follows:

> *"I agree that the process seems to take a long time. I am sure you would agree that your priority is to get this fixed."*

Tactic 48: Give Away Something

Sometimes an angry person wants to feel he has "won a battle". The smart employee will look for things to give away, or give in on, to give the impression that the customer is gaining "something".

The question to ask yourself is: <u>"Is there something the customer wants that I can provide?"</u>

We need to be careful with this one. We don't want to reward bad behavior by giving in, so we need to use this tactic only when the client is behaving politely. For example, a customer who is yelling while waiting in a line is actually rewarded if we serve that person out of turn. We don't want to reward bad behavior.

If you look back on our Internet example earlier in the chapter, do you think that if the employee offered a small discount on the overage charge, that it would have really made an impression on the customer? Of course it would. Not only would it allow him to save a few dollars, but he can now go to his wife and explain how he got the company to reduce the charge.

Of course, that assumes the employee had the authority to do that, or could get the authority, but it's just smart business, particularly in an industry where there is a high level of competition, and customer retention is so important.

Conclusion

We've just scratched the surface talking about problem solving, which includes elements of negotiation and conflict management. We have provided you with some concrete tactics that you can use during this phase. Remember that problem solving will be ineffective if the customer is too angry to listen and think properly. If so, use acknowledgement tactics to calm the person down, before proceeding to the actual problem.

Chapter XIV — Assertive Limit Setting

We try to use "gentle" and indirect techniques to defuse hostile clients, but sometimes we need to set and enforce limits on hostile behavior. In this chapter we guide you through the process of setting and enforcing reasonable limits regarding customer behavior.

INTRODUCTION

So far, you've learned almost fifty tactics for dealing with and defusing hostile people. For the most part these tactics are "gentle", subtle, and use the least possible "force". That is in line with our principle that we only use stronger tactics after we have determined that our more subtle techniques have not worked.

There will be times when the gentler techniques don't work. What do you do when you spend time trying to defuse a client who just won't calm down, and won't stop behaving badly? What do you do when a client is consistently over the line that separates angry behavior from totally unacceptable behavior?

That's where assertive limit setting comes in. Setting limits is a stronger approach to dealing with hostile people and is based on the premise that YOU also have rights. While we recognize that a customer has some leeway in expressing his anger, you also have the right to feel safe, and to end interactions when the other person's behavior is grossly inappropriate.

 Snapshot

When?
Assertive limit setting is appropriate in 2 situations. **First**, it is used to begin to end a conversation when you have determined that further conversation is not going to accomplish anything. Generally, you make this determination based on: **a)** the individual's behavior and **b)** having tried other gentler defusing techniques. **Second,** limit setting is used to try to get the customer to modify his behavior so you can work together to build some sort of positive resolution.

How you do it is important. If you allow yourself to get triggered, and lose your temper, you are likely to respond in an angry way, which may make the situation worse. However, if you follow the strategy of assertive limit setting, you will be handling the situation in a strong, polite way that makes it clear that you will not accept the behaviors the hostile person is exhibiting.

ASSERTIVE LIMIT SETTING

Assertive limit setting is appropriate in two situations. First, you can use limits to end a conversation when you have determined that further conversation is not going to accomplish anything. Generally, you decide to do so based on a) **the individual's behavior** and b) **failure of gentler defusing techniques.** Second, you can use limit setting to encourage the customer to modify their behavior, so you can work together to build some sort of positive resolution.

Each of us has limits in terms of what we are willing to accept from an angry customer. Limit setting is a way to communicate our limits to the client, in the hope that he/she will modify his/her behavior so it is more constructive for both participants.

DEFINITION AND FORMAT

Let's define an assertive limit setting statement. An assertive limit setting statement conveys to the individual:

1. that certain behaviors are unacceptable

2. a request to change those behaviors (usually implied)

3. an indication of the consequences that will occur if the customer does not alter their behavior

4. a question that gives the client the choice regarding what happens next

Let's look at an example:

> *"Sir, if you continue to swear and yell* **(1),** *I will have to end our conversation* **(3).**
> *Would you prefer to continue or stop now?"* **(4)**

The first sentence **(1)** indicates the specific behaviors that are problematic. The part labeled **(3)** indicates the consequence that will occur if the behavior does not change, while the portion labeled **(4)** is a question that indicates that the client has the option of choosing whether the conversation continues or not. You will notice that the request for behavior is not made explicitly, but will be understood.

Let's take each of the components in turn.

TACTIC 49: DESCRIBE UNACCEPTABLE BEHAVIOR

If we want the customer to change his behavior, we need to be specific as to the behaviors that are unacceptable, and/or the behavior we want the customer to use.

This means that when we describe behavior we MUST be specific in our descriptions. Don't say:

> *"Sir, unless you calm down, I will have to end our conversation".*

This isn't specific enough, and does not refer to specific behavior. If you say something like the above you are likely to get the following response:

> *"Calm down!? Calm down? You think I'm not calm?!"* [and so on]

By not being specific you are MORE likely to provide ammunition to the hostile person, something you don't want to do. Besides, the problem isn't that the person isn't calm — the problem is that the customer is swearing and yelling. Even if the customer remains "uncalm", if the swearing and yelling stops, that solves the immediate problem.

The most important part of setting limits is to describe specific behaviors rather than vague non-behaviors.

Tactic 50: Request Behavior Change

You want to convey to the customer that you are requesting that he cease doing what he is doing, and do something else. There are two ways of doing this. One is to make an explicit request. For example:

> "I would appreciate it if you would stop yelling."

The second is to have the request implicit. That means that you don't make a specific verbal request. Instead, you phrase things so that your meaning is clear. When you say:

> "If you continue to swear and yell, I will have to end the conversation…"

the customer knows you are making a request to stop swearing and yelling.

Which approach is better? In most cases, the second is a better approach. Why? Remember that in the section on verbal self-defense we mentioned that using "I" statements may create additional argument. An angry customer is not particularly interested in "what you appreciate", and using that language can create additional anger and hostility. By making your request, and beginning with the word "I", you create the impression that you are focusing on your own motives, and not trying to help the customer. That's creates a higher risk of backlash.

While we want the customer to know that we are asking for a change in behavior, we prefer to use an indirect implicit approach.

Tactic 51: State Consequences

You need to make it clear to the customer what will happen if he continues to behave inappropriately, or in a way that "crosses your line". The best way to state this is in an IF — THEN format.

> *"If you continue to yell, I will end the conversation"* or

> *"If you don't stop pounding the table, I will ask you to leave"*

Now, there are a few things to keep in mind when stating consequences.

1. Use Cooperative Language

Don't use language that is confrontational (Type I language). That means avoiding things like:

> *…. I will throw you out.*

.... You will be arrested.

It means staying away from "hot words". It means using "we" instead of :"I", when possible. It means applying the other concepts of language use we have covered.

2. USE ENFORCEABLE CONSEQUENCES

Don't set limits or consequences that you are unable or unwilling to enforce. When you set limits and state consequences, you **MUST** be prepared to enforce them. If you do not, you lose credibility and control.

Snapshot

Natural Consequence vs. Punishment

When you talk about or enforce a consequence keep clear in your mind that this is not a punishment or getting even. A consequence is a natural outcome of somebody's action, like getting wet if you walk in the rain.

TACTIC 52: OFFER CHOICE

There is a difference between punishing someone, and applying consequences. The difference is that when you punish someone, it is the punisher who uses power. When you apply consequences, the power appears more shared. That is, it's clear that the other person has a choice. **IF** the behavior stops, things will continue. If the customer chooses not to stop the offensive behavior, the customer also chooses that consequence —ending the conversation.

The difference is important because if the customer feels that you are punishing her by using power, she will rebel/respond with increased force. If she realizes she has choices, and still has some control over the outcome, she is less likely to be more aggressive.

For this reason we want to be clear that we are offering a choice to the customer. So we say:

"Would you like to continue or stop now? "It's up to you whether we continue."
"We can continue if you stop [behavior], or you can return some other time."

Notice how the statements above don't sound personal? Compare with *"If you continue I will throw you out?"* which sounds like a personal threat. That's why you try to make it clear that the person has a choice.

TACTIC 53: ENFORCING LIMITS

Obviously, there isn't much point in setting limits if you aren't going to enforce them. Again, the way you enforce the limits is very important. For example:

Employee: *"Sir, if you continue to swear, I am going to ask you to leave".* [Limit Setting]

Customer ignores and continues.

Employee: *"Sir, I warned you. Now get out right now."* [Limit enforcement]

Not so good! In this example, the limit enforcement statement has a threatening tone (*I warned you*) and an order which sounds emotional, personal and punishing. (*Now get out right now*). The employee's limit enforcement statement may cause the person to become even more aggressive.

We want to enforce our limits in a calm way, again using cooperative Type 2 language, rather than confrontational language.

Enforcing limits contains the following parts.

(1)   Reference to the limits stated previously.

(2)   A request to comply with the consequence.

(3)   An offer for further help.

For example:

> *"Sir, I explained to you that I won't continue this conversation if you continue to yell (1). I am ending this discussion now (2), but you are welcome to come back some other time." (3)*

The first part **(1)** refers to the earlier limit. You will note that we don't use the word warn, or anything similar. The reason is that when we say "I warned you" it sounds like a threat—like a personal issue or attack.

The second sentence **(2)** involves stating that the consequence is being applied, and is also an implicit gentle request for the customer to comply. The third component **(3)** is the offer of further help. Why do we do this?

We want to send the message that our concern is not with the person as a human being, but with that person's behavior. We also want to convey that we **WILL** try to help, and we are not permanently cutting off the customer. By adding this statement, we show that we are not making this a personal issue and we are not forcing the customer into a corner.

Snapshot

Behavior, Not Person
We want to send the message that our concern is not with the person as a human being, but with that person's behavior. We also want to convey that we **will** try to help, and we are not permanently cutting the customer off.

One more note about the third component. When you suggest that the person can come back at some other time, don't say:

"You are welcome to come back <u>when you calm down</u>."

While this may seem like a reasonable thing to say, it tends to come across as patronizing and is not much different than the following statements:

- ♦   *"You are welcome to come back when you get a grip."*

- ♦   *"You are welcome to come back when you smarten up."*

- *"You are welcome to come back if you act responsibly."*

These are patronizing and offensive. Don't do it.

THEN WHAT HAPPENS?

Assume you have set some limits, and these limits are ignored. You then enforce those limits by requesting something, or stating that you are ending the conversation. One of two things is going to happen. The customer will comply (e.g. leave), or the customer will not comply. If the customer responds positively (complies), you are pretty much done. But what if the customer won't leave?

This is the point where you must be very careful. Your reaction will depend on the situation. If the person is in your office, and you ask him to leave and are refused, avoid a "head-to-head" confrontation.

Provided the individual is not a physical threat, you can offer another choice. Look at the following example which takes place in the employee's office.

> **Employee:** *"Sir, if you continue to yell, I am going to have to end this conversation. It's up to you whether you want to continue."*

> Customer continues to yell.

> **Employee:** *"I explained to you that I won't continue if you yell. I'm going to end this conversation, but you are welcome to come back some other time."*

> **Customer:** *"So you want me to leave? I'm not going anywhere. Just try to make me go."*

> **Employee:** *"Sir, I'm not going to force you to leave. It's really up to you what happens next. However, I'm stepping out. If you want to stay here for a little while to think, that's fine. However, if you aren't gone in twenty minutes, we will have to contact security (police) to escort you out of the office. It's up to you."*

Now, notice what the employee has done:

- She has reassured the client that there will be no physical confrontation initiated by the employee.

- She gives up something by saying the client can stay for some reasonable period of time.

- She highlights the issue of choice.

- She then states another consequence (security).

- Throughout the whole set of statements, she uses cooperative language, and stresses choice.

Now to continue, in ten or fifteen minutes the employee returns to the office door and says:

Employee: *"Mr. Jones, have you decided what you want to do next?"*

Customer: *"I wanna talk some more."*

Employee: *"OK, are we agreed that the yelling will stop?"*

Customer: *"OK"*

Employee: *"OK, we can talk some more provided there is no yelling."*

In this situation the customer realized that the employee was in control of the interaction and he chose to alter his behavior.

If the customer responds negatively, then the employee can call security if that option is available. If not, then the employee needs to notify a manager of the problem.. At that point the employee's role is ended, and he shouldn't take part in the removal process.

What happens if you don't have access to security personnel? You have a few choices. You can return with a few co-workers and make a request for the person to leave. Unfortunately, this is confrontational. Sometimes it works, some times not ... high risk-high gain. Remember that you never know whether a person is carrying a weapon of some sort. Trying to intimidate a person into leaving is not a good choice.

 **CAUTION!**

Safety First
It is not your job to physically restrain or remove a customer (unless you are in law enforcement). You aren't trained, or paid to do so. Don't let yourself be goaded into thinking you should physically handle a customer.

Remember one thing. **It isn't your job to "throw someone out".** It's dangerous, so don't get involved in it. If a person refuses to leave, then often it is best to exit the situation, inform your colleagues and boss, and just let the person cool off alone.

Chapter Conclusion

Setting and enforcing limits is an important part of the defusing hostility process. But you **MUST** be aware that limit setting and enforcement will work effectively when you do it correctly, and may blow up in your face if you sound punishing, and power oriented.

This page left blank intentionally

Chapter XVI — For Managers & Supervisors

INTRODUCTION

In the previous chapters, we have outlined almost fifty tactics to defuse hostility, but we haven't specifically addressed the behavior and roles that managers and supervisors can play in the process.

Since managers and supervisors deal with hostile customers, what we have already discussed also applies to them. However managers also play other roles in the organization and have additional responsibilities. Specifically these additional responsibilities relate to the following:

1. Reinforcing the use of defusing strategies on the part of employees.

2. Ensuring the work environment is as safe as possible.

3. Communicating safety policy to staff.

4. Communicating / explaining other important policies to staff.

5. Reversing staff decisions.

Let's take a look at some specific tactics.

Reinforcing Defusing Tactics

Managers/supervisors can influence the degree to which staff use defusing strategies. Keep in mind that the manager/supervisor plays a leadership role in the organization. Staff take their cues regarding appropriate and inappropriate behavior from the people above them in the organization.

TACTIC 54: MODEL APPROPRIATE BEHAVIOR

The best way to encourage staff to use professional and effective methods for dealing with hostile customers is to model the behavior you want them to use. If you treat staff and customers the way you want your staff to treat customers, staff will realize that this is the "standard" of behavior. If, however, you treat staff and employees in ways that increase hostility, staff will pick up on your behavior. And, it is your behavior that sets the standard, not just your words.

 Bet You Didn't Know

Employees Take Cues From YOU
Employees take their cues about what constitutes desirable work behavior from their managers. They learn from you. If you treat employees and customers well, and deal with difficult situations with grace and a firm but gentle touch, employees will tend to see this as what THEY should do. If you treat staff roughly, they will tend to emulate your behavior, and that doesn't help anyone.

TACTIC 55: SUPPORT SKILL BUILDING

Snapshot

Learning Culture
Support learning and provide opportunities for staff to improve their work related skills including defusing angry customers. Learning need not be formal, as in going to training. You can teach. You can help them learn from each other. There's many low cost ways to create a learning culture.

Apart from modeling defusing tactics, managers can also create a climate where skill building can occur. For example, managers can support staff in attending seminars on defusing hostility and/or customer service. Or, managers can encourage staff to talk about difficult customers at staff meetings, so staff can learn from each other. The latter can be particularly useful, and is a practice adopted by some of my clients.

At regularly scheduled staff meetings, set aside a short period of time (e.g.. fifteen minutes) to discuss a hostile "case" that has occurred. One person presents the case to the rest of the group, and people can brain-storm around other strategies that can be used. Or, the case can be a "success story", where a staff member shares what worked well.

TACTIC 56: DEBRIEFING WITH STAFF

Managers can play a teaching role by debriefing when hostile situations occur. For example, if a hostile customer is referred to the manager, rather than simply forgetting about the incident, it makes sense for the manager to sit down with the employee to discuss how he/she handled it, and to provide information about how the manager handled it. This need not be a long process or a formal, unpleasant one. The best tone to take is one that stresses learning and prevention.

If you are going to debrief staff, it is important that it become an "organizational habit", so staff don't feel they are being singled out. To work towards creating a learning tone, be prepared with questions to ask the employee, such as:

- ◆   Describe the customers behavior.
- ◆   How did you react?
- ◆   What seemed effective/ineffective.
- ◆   What would you do differently.
- ◆   How do you feel now?

You can also describe the process you used with the customer. You can make a few suggestions for future situations, but make sure you are specific, and refer to the employee's behavior, not him/her as a person. And only make one or two suggestions so the employee doesn't feel overwhelmed.

Make sure that it is clear that you are working with the employee to avoid future unpleasant situations, that you are playing a supportive coaching role, rather than a "judging" role.

WORK ENVIRONMENT SAFETY

Managers have a major responsibility to ensure that the environment is as safe as possible. Often this will involve looking at the environment to make sure that it is arranged so that it promotes safety for both staff and customers.

In a later chapter on safety, we will suggest some environmental variable that you can look at.

TACTIC 57: CONDUCT A SAFETY AUDIT

A safety audit is a process where you examine your environment and policies to ensure that they support creating the safest work environment possible. Safety audits are commonly undertaken with respect to the workplace, but can also address how field workers carry out their responsibilities. For example, one client determined that safety for field workers could be enhanced by making cellular phones available to staff, and creating a standardized calling process so that the "home office" was aware of where the employee was, and who he/she was dealing with.

 Bet You Didn't Know

Workplace Safety
Even if you work in a company that has Workplace, Safety and Health officers, workplace safety is STILL part of the managerial and supervisory responsibility. You MUST take an active role in doing everything possible to protect your staff, customers and property, and yes, that extends to dealing with angry customers.

You can undertake a safety audit yourself, but we suggest that you make use of law enforcement agencies and the services they provide. Often your local law enforcement agency can make suggestions about how to arrange your office space, and suggest other things you can do to maximize the physical safety of all concerned. A good place to start is with the community relations division of your local police force.

Remember that a safety audit includes two components — an evaluation of the physical environment, and an evaluation of existing policies and procedures that may impact on safety.

TACTIC 58: CREATE POLICY ON VIOLENCE

One of the hardest parts of dealing with hostile people, particularly those extreme in their behavior, is determining what one can and should do. Some of my clients have chosen to develop a written policy that explains to staff what they are expected to do in particular situations. This reduces the ambiguity and stress experienced by staff. It is a step that I recommend to ALL companies that deal with customers.

Policies vary, of course, but generally they include some or all of the following:

- ♦ when staff can terminate service
- ♦ how staff are expected to communicate termination of service
- ♦ when staff should request backup (security, police, etc.)

- how staff should request backup
- how threats should be handled
- when management should be involved
- when it is appropriate to use "panic buttons"
- reporting forms (incident reports)

One of the best ways to create your own policy is to contact other organizations that may have done this. It is fairly easy to adapt someone else's policy to your situation. However you go about it, your policy should be relatively short, not require huge amounts of paperwork, and be unambiguous. And, it should reflect the experience of those "on the line". Don't develop a policy of this sort without extensive consultation with front line staff.

TACTIC 59: COMMUNICATE SAFETY POLICY

You would think it would be fairly clear that simply creating a violence in the workplace policy is not sufficient and that each employee needs to understand it. Communication is obviously important. My experience is that a good number of organizations develop excellent policies on the subject but fall short when it comes to communication. Even in organizations that have had such policies in place for several years, I find a good number of people who don't know what the policy means, or have found that when they follow the policy, they get hassled by management.

Snapshot

Policy Not Enough
A safety policy is important, but it's not enough. It must be communicated to and supported by everyone in the organization. It must be followed and enforced. That's management's responsibility.

One organization developed a policy, and installed "panic buttons" at front counters. The policy stated that when an employee felt a potential for physical harm, they were to hit their panic button, and this would summon additional personnel or security.

Unfortunately, the manager of the installation made it clear that staff were NOT to follow this policy unless the threat was immediate and obvious. He said something to the effect of *"You'd better have a damn good reason for using it."* At the same time, staff were encouraged NOT to file incident reports, and NOT to summon the police when necessary, because these actions created "huge paperwork 'hassles'.

Not surprisingly, staff were confused and angry about the manager's clear violation of corporate policy. In this case the problem was that the manager had not understood that he was expected to implement the policy as written, and that this would be considered part of his job. The problem was inadequate communication to and from the manager.

This is an extreme case. More often the policy is developed and circulated in writing, to be forgotten the next week. We suggest that the policy be discussed at meetings when it is introduced. We also suggest that the policy be discussed in an ongoing way during the first year. Managers can revisit the policy during staff meetings, requesting input, comments, and real life experiences about how it is working. This makes the policy come to life, and says to employees that management is taking its safety obligations seriously.

TACTIC 60: COMMUNICATING/EXPLAINING OTHER POLICIES TO STAFF

An important aspect of defusing hostility is the ability to explain WHY certain decisions have been made. We have discussed this in the chapter on problem-solving, but just to reiterate, angry customers need to know that your decisions are not made arbitrarily, and that rules and regulations serve some purpose. People defusing hostile people need to be able to explain to clients the reasons behind decisions, or to provide information.

Now, in order for staff to be able to explain things to clients, they need to understand the reasoning behind policies and regulations. Sadly, not all employees know why things are done a particular way. So it is important that the reasoning behind policies and procedures be clear to staff so they can convey them intelligently to customers.

Nothing annoys customers more than a staff member who can't explain the reasoning of a decision, or the thinking behind a procedure.

We suggest that staff be periodically "re-oriented" about policies and procedures, and the reasons for them. And, of course, when things are changed, it must be clear to staff, why changes have been made.

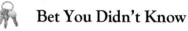 **Bet You Didn't Know**

Clarity? Not Likely
Policies and procedures often seem straight forward to those that draft them. When real people try to apply a policy to real life situations, that's when ambiguities and gray areas show up. Do not assume that staff understand how the policy applies to any given situation. Work through examples with staff to clarify the application of policy. This IS important.

Remember that a well-informed employee who understands why things are done will be better able to defuse frustrated clients.

TACTIC 61: EFFECTIVE REVERSING OF EMPLOYEE DECISIONS

There are times when a manager will reverse a staff member's decision. Sometimes it will be because the employee has made an error, but more often reversals are a result of a judgement call on the part of the manager.

Reversing a decision, when the reversal benefits the client, can be an effective way to terminate a hostile situation. However, you need to know that reversals must be done effectively.

First, be aware that reversing a decision may appear like you are rewarding undesirable client behavior. We don't want to grease the squeaky wheel too often. When reversing a decision, it should be clear why you are doing so.

Second, be aware that it can be frustrating for staff to have their decisions reversed. A common problem is that managers don't take the time to explain why a decision has been reversed, so employees feel their competence is being questioned. Make it clear to the employee why you changed the decision.

Chapter Summary

We have discussed a number of tactics related to how management can support staff in dealing with hostile clients. Don't underestimate the importance of the management role. Non-supportive managers who communicate inconsistently can seriously affect the ability of staff to deal with difficult customers, while effective managers can be a valuable asset to staff, reducing the "fall-out" from mishandled hostile situations.

We suggest that managers and supervisors complete the following checklist of responsibilities and actions.

MANAGER/SUPERVISOR CHECKLIST

Task	Yes	Not Yet
I have ensured my staff are well trained in defusing hostility.		
I model appropriate defusing behavior when dealing with customers.		
I model appropriate defusing behavior when dealing with staff.		
I use staff meetings to discuss difficult defusing cases.		
I debrief staff after difficult defusing situations.		
I publicly recognize when an employee defuses a difficult customer.		
I coach my staff to help build their defusing skills.		
I privately congratulate employees when they defuse effectively.		
I have initiated a yearly safety audit.		
I have invited law enforcement to talk to staff about safety.		
We have a written policy on safety/violence		
I have ensured that staff and management understand the safety policy.		
I have obtained input about the safety policy from staff.		
When I reverse an employee decision, I explain the reasoning to staff		
I ensure that staff understand reasons behind regulations and policy.		
I have developed my own defusing hostility skills.		

Chapter XVI—Customer Interactions Through Media

Increasing amounts of interactions with customers occur using various technologies, from the telephone and e-mail to the use of "social media" such as Twitter and Facebook. In this chapter we'll provide suggestions as to how these can be used effectively. Because marketing, sales and customer service tend to merge into one tangled ball of twine, particularly on social networks, we'll go a little farther afield in this chapter, to help you understand the newer media.

INTRODUCTION

Customers and organizations have become increasingly reliant on the use of technology to make communication easier and more convenient, although it's arguable whether those that serve customers, or the customers themselves, are better off as a result.. Telephones are the mainstay technology that has dominated communication for many decades, but additional add-ons such as voice mail now help and/or hinder effective customer service. E-mail is another tool that has emerged as a standard communication tool and is now accepted as a "normal" way to interact.

More recently, particularly in the decade beginning in 2010, "social media" or "social networks" have emerged as gathering places for people -- for customers. Web site based systems like Twitter, Facebook, LinkedIn and many more have made it possible for every person to have the potential to communicate with many others. Blogs, wikis, and video and picture sharing sites allow anyone who wishes to have a voice -- and now anyone can share an opinion. That does NOT mean everyone is heard, though.

Organizations, recognizing these platforms may have potential for both commercial gain and commercial loss, have started moving into these spaces. For this reason, we need to address how to use media effectively, particularly within the context of dealing with dissatisfied or angry customers.

 Snapshot

Customers Being Heard?
Blogs, wikis, and video and picture sharing sites allow anyone who wishes to have a voice -- and now anyone can share an opinion. That doesn't mean every angry customer gets heard. Most don't.

BEFORE WE EVEN START!

Before we even begin to discuss how to deal effectively with customers through various media, there's is one critical point to cover.

> You must know what your organization expects of you regarding your participation and use of media as it pertains to your job. In particular, you must know what you are NOT allowed to do.

More and more organizations in commercial and public sectors are realizing that they need to present unified and coherent messages about themselves to their customers. Having a number of employees giving out information (and often differing information) via media confuses customers, and can result in people becoming more upset. For that reason many organizations develop policies that explain what you can and cannot do or say, particularly if you represent yourself as an employee of the organization. Many people have lost their jobs across all sectors as a result of saying the "wrong" things on the Internet.

It is a given that organizations will become more and more concerned about the use of social media by employees, and whether it's good or bad, fair or otherwise, you need to know and understand what is permissible, and where you might fit in terms of communicating publicly about your employer. So find out. Human resources is often a good place to start, and of course, you can ask your supervisor. Regardless, find out whether your organization has a social media policy.

UNDERSTANDING THE CHANGES PUSHED BY THE NEW MEDIA

With respect to customer service, the new media, (social networks) impacts how organizations see customer service. It's always been the case that a dissatisfied customer would communicate his or her anger about service or product quality to many more people than will the happy customer, or at least that's been the "accepted wisdom". Now, because everyone has a voice, or the potential to loudly voice an opinion, there has been a merging of three things: Customer service, marketing and branding, and reputation management are converging into one. Traditionally, each has been a separate field, and each has been ensconced in a different departmental area. As they merge, the skills needed on the part of customer service representatives will expand.

What, you ask, does this have to do with you? You don't market. You don't worry about branding. For goodness sake, why try to manage corporate reputation when the company itself seems hell-bent on looking bad anyway?

You are the employee who deals directly with the public. If you operate as a customer service contact, you will be expected to deal with angry customers in various media -- media that are also used to market and present a positive image to the public. That's becoming more important, not just for your employer, but also for you.

Anything that negatively affects people's perceptions of your employer has the potential to affects you.

Social media platforms allow the spreading of bad experiences quickly. That is why organizations are looking to be more active on these platforms to try to improve communication and customer service, and manage the discussions. While that may not yet be part of your customer service job, that could change. While it really isn't even POSSIBLE to manage those discussion, organizations are trying, and you will be expected to try. You'll also be expected **not to screw up** when you operate on social media sites.

THE EFFECT OF THE MEDIUM

Before we discuss the various technologies and media by which you communicate with customers now, or may use in the near future, here's an important point. **When the medium changes, so does communication**. Here's a simple example. When you talk to a loved one on the phone and say: *"I'll see you tomorrow"* is it the same as standing together, face to face and saying the identical thing? It IS the same words, right?

Bet You Didn't Know

Even The Research Is Bad
Most research on customer service and social media is done via survey, and not by observing actual consumer behavior. People assume that customers do what they say they do, and we know that that is simply not true in many cases. In Social Psychology it's long been understood that what people say and what they do can be quite different. That's why almost all of the customer service/social media research is terribly misleading and gives an overly optimistic picture.

It's not just the words that communicate. Media differ in terms of the "sub-channels" they include and the diversity of information they can convey, with face to face interactions being the richest. More is communicated in person than on the telephone, which, in turn is different from, let's say, e-mail. This alters how you use the different media. As another example, consider the differences between television and radio. The skills needed to come across well on television are quite different than those required to come across well on the radio.

The medium alters the message. Just as importantly, different messages are suited for different media. Part of dealing with customers now involves choosing the RIGHT medium for the problem. This idea hasn't fully penetrated into the heads of those that claim that social media contacts will replace email and the telephone in terms of providing customer service and dealing with irate customers. Blogs, Facebook and Twitter have so many severe limitations that they simply are not suitable for most customer service related conversations.

Let's begin by discussing the most familiar medium (besides face to face) for interacting with angry and difficult customers -- the telephone.

TELEPHONE COMMUNICATION

Many employees deal with hostile customers on the phone. Some feel that hostile people are easier to deal with via a phone, while others feel that hostile people are more difficult on the telephone. Here are some things to consider.

First, there is a tendency for hostile people to be MORE abusive in telephone conversations. The reason is that they don't see you as a person, but as a disembodied voice. People WILL say things on the telephone that they wouldn't say if they were standing in front of you. It's that "depersonalization" process.

Second, one advantage of telephone conversations is that you do not face an immediate physical threat. This may allow you to feel less intimidated, although with the advent of cell phones, you don't know if the person on the phone is 10 feet away from you.

Third, because telephones involve only voice communication, you may need to adopt a different, stronger tone than you would in person. That is because you can't use non-verbal tactics (e.g.. body language) to take control of the interaction.

Fourth, remember that you have more control over phone conversations as compared to in person discussions. You can hang up at any time, without dealing with the issue of whether the customer is going to leave. Then again, the person can call back!

Here's a summary of advantages and disadvantages of telephone based communication:

Advantages	Disadvantages
You have more control (terminate discussion)	Person can keep calling, you probably still need to answer
Provides extra feeling of safety from violence	Poor medium for communicating bad news or with emotional people since there is no non-verbal feedback.
Conversation is not available to a lot of other people/onlookers	Difficult to communicate with more than one person (e.g. a couple or family if that's required)
Interaction does not require travel for you or customer, making it more convenient	As with face-to-face, details tend to get lost, so not effective on its own if issues are complex
	Tendency for customers to be more abusive due to perception of anonymity
	Can attract chronic nuisance callers who just like to complain or are lonely
Table 16.1 Advantages/Disadvantages of Telephones	

TACTIC 62: USE A STRONGER TONE

When trying to gain control of a telephone conversation, speak more loudly than you would in person. This doesn't mean yelling, but it may mean raising your voice so you can be heard. Louder volume should NOT be accompanied by an angry tone, or one that communicates frustration.

TACTIC 63: USE A VERY QUIET VOLUME

Using a louder tone of voice can work to gain control, but so can speaking quietly. This forces the client to listen. If you try a louder tone and it is ineffective, try speaking very very quietly, so your words are barely audible to the other person. This may be enough to cause the person to pause, and ask you to repeat yourself, returning control to you.

TACTIC 64: USE MORE OBVIOUS WORD STRESSES

In a face-to-face interaction your non-verbal behavior is used to accent the important parts of what you are saying. On the phone you can't do this. You may want to accent your words in a different, more obvious way.

Let's look at the following sentences. Try to hear the differences in word stress. When you come to a capitalized word, that means that the word is emphasized or stressed.

 CAUTION!

Phone OOPSIES
Many an employee has suffered the slings and arrows after having made some snarky comment about a customer on hold, only to discover the customer could hear everything that was said.

> *Sir, I must have your name in order to help you.*

Note we haven't capitalized any words to indicate heavy emphasis. When spoken this might sound OK, but it also might come off as disinterested due to the mild or non-existent word.

Look at this example.

> *Sir, I MUST have your NAME in order to HELP you.*

The capitalized words are the ones that are stressed. This pattern conveys energy and conviction due to the heavier emphasis on some of the words. It comes across as "something to pay attention to". On the phone, you probably want to use the next example, though.

Now, the third example.

> *SIR, I MUST have your NAME, in order to HELP you.*

In this example, we emphasize an extra word (SIR), and emphasize the stressed words more heavily. (the capitalized words). This slightly stronger set of stresses is more appropriate on the phone. One tip -- don't emphasis too many words in a sentence, since this will sound angry. Better to put extra stress on fewer words.

It's hard to convey word stress patterns on paper. Try to "hear" the differences by saying the examples out loud.

TACTIC 65: ALWAYS SUMMARIZE

So much information gets lost or distorted in both face to face and telephone conversations. The fact that you have discussed an issue with the customer, and seemingly agreed, does not mean that you both understood the conversation in the same way.

Therefore at the end of any phone conversation take a few seconds to summarize what you said, and what the customer said, and any agreements made, including actions each can or will take. It sounds like this:

> *"So, let me recap. I'm going to send you a new copy of your bank statement, and you've promised to make sure the overdraft is paid before April 2nd. Is that how you see it?"*

If you discover that you and the customer have a different understanding of the conversations and any agreements, then resolve the differences before ending the call.

Snapshot

Summarize!
At the end of any phone conversation take a few seconds to summarize what you said, and what the customer said, and any agreements made, including actions each can or will take. Check that your understanding matches the customer's understanding. You'll be amazed how many problems this prevents.

TACTIC 66: USE FOLLOW UPS/WRITTEN NOTE WHEN POSSIBLE

Verbal summaries can reduce misunderstanding and future conflict with customers, but there is no substitute for the printed word (paper or e-mail) as a means of summarizing a conversation. Written follow ups are important when there is any significant degree of detail the customer must be aware of, including dates, times, specific regulations, contact names, and so forth.

Following up with details can be very effective in reducing misunderstandings or at least catching them before they blow up, but of course, there is the practical issue of time.

Do your best given the time and practical constraints you may have. Preventing situations that spawn angry customers is even better than defusing them! Written summaries prevent misunderstandings that, left unrecognized, can create conflict.

TACTIC 67: USE OTHER RELEVANT TACTICS

Almost all of the tactics that relate to verbal behavior work equally well on the phone or in person. The CARP system applies, as do verbal self-defense techniques, acknowledgment techniques, disengaging, etc. In particular, be prepared to set limits and enforce them, being sure to let the customer know that he or she is welcome to call back when ready to abide by the limits you have set. This is because it's often not possible for an employee to "refuse service" to a customer without incurring the wrath of a manager.

TACTIC 68: TELEPHONE SILENCE REVISITED

Tactic 28 (Telephone Silence) was described in Chapter VIII, as a means of gaining control of a telephone interaction. It's included here because it is SO important.

When a customer will not stop talking on the phone long enough for you to get a word in edgewise or obtain even the basic information you need to try to help, you MUST get the person to be quiet, or it's all a waste of time. If you interrupt, it tends to increase the length of time the customer talks, since he or she restarts the rant from the beginning.

The solution is to be completely silent. Make sure no sounds reaches the microphone in the phone, or at least, as little sound as possible. Relatively quickly, the customer will eventually ask *"Are you there?"* At this point you respond, take control of the conversation, and use the rest of the CARP model. It doesn't work all the time, but then again, nothing does.

TACTIC 69: CHRONIC NUISANCE CALLER TACTIC

Since calling on the phone is so easy, some people will call repeatedly to voice their concerns, or because they are lonely. Often such callers don't have any particular issue that can be dealt with through problem-solving, and they can eat up lots of time because they call so often.

 Wise Thoughts To Ponder

Chronic Callers & Loneliness
These days it's hard to be elderly, or isolated from people, and many in our society are. It's not uncommon for lonely people to call a company just to talk. Is this a real imposition — to help someone needing to hear a cheery voice. Something worth thinking about.

Companies/your employer may frown on "cutting someone off" completely by refusing to answer their phone calls, and you can't really "order" them to stop calling. In effect the only things you can do, besides dodging phone calls (which isn't recommended) are a) to elicit their cooperation and b) to set and enforce assertively constructed limits.

Often, chronic callers are fairly pleasant, so you can request, suggest or assert that one call per [day, week] is all you can handle, but that you would be happy to spend a few minutes talking if it's once a [day, week]. Then if the person calls more often, or the caller tries to extend each call beyond a minute or two, apply limits and enforce them. Eventually, your chronic caller will "learn the rules" and abide by them, and/or call somewhere else for his or her conversations.

Certainly, it's understandable if this doesn't fit your busy schedule, and if you have many chronic callers, you aren't going to be able to give this "service" to callers. However, keep in mind that you don't have the control to never answer the calls of chronic callers or to hang up on them. If you do either, you may be called on the carpet yourself. Investing a little time once in a while may be preferable to creating a situation where there is head to head open conflict.

If the chronic caller is calling about a specific issue -- an issue you cannot help him or her with, then look to redirect the person to talk to someone who has more authority (Redirect tactic). Offer a phone number if possible, or an address (e-mail or otherwise), and do so courteously. Consider asking the person to call you back in a week or two to let you know how it all turned out.

If you have an "over-caller", someone who calls repeatedly in a short time for someone else in the office who is unavailable, here's what to do.

> **Caller:** *Is George Pappas in?*
>
> **Employee:** *No, he's still away from his desk. Is this Ms. Meriwether calling?*
>
> **Caller:** *Yes, it is. Why is he never in his office, or is he dodging my calls? I need to talk to him urgently, and he's not calling back.*
>
> **Employee:** (1) *I can see you are pretty concerned, so here's what I can do.* (2) *I handle all of Mr. Pappas messages, and I promise you that I will give this to him personally, by hand, and let him know that you'd like to speak to him immediately.* (3) *I know he's very busy today, so let me set up an appointment for a phone call. I'll call you at 3:30 on the dot, and that way you don't have to sit by the phone all day.* (4) *How's that sound?*

In (1) the employee acknowledges the caller's feelings and concerns. In (2), assurances are given and a promise, and in (3) the employee offers to solve the immediate problem of getting the two connected. In (4) the employee uses a question to provide a sense of choice.

Of course, what you say will depend on what commitments you can reasonably make. If the person continues to call back, then return to the promise, set assertive limits, enforce them, and end the conversation with "*Mrs. Meriwether, I'll speak to you at 3:30. Bye for now*"

TACTIC 70: HAVING AND USING REFERRAL RESOURCES

 Wise Thoughts To Ponder

Not Your Job?
Maybe not, but just because someone contacts you for help that has nothing to do with your job, does it mean you shouldn't help? Consider whether taking a few extra minutes to help someone might be good for you and good for your employer.

It's common to have callers who have been told to call you on a particular issue, or think you are the person to call, when, in fact, you have nothing to do with the issue. Those callers can be unruly because they will feel they have been given the runaround, or false information. Rather than simply saying you can't help, the proper approach is to have a list of contacts in other internal departments or (external) companies to whom you can refer the individual. Having a list of referral contacts for handy for recurring situations is a good idea.

For example, let's say you work a realtor's office. You could y get a call from a homeless person wanting to know the location of the nearest hostel, something clearly has nothing to do with real estate. If you have a list of available places, even though hostels do not fall under the bailiwick of your department, you can be of help, and avoid a drawn out conversation as the frustrated person chews you out. Best of all you know you've helped.

Communication Via E-mail

For many people and companies, e-mail has supplanted paper letters for many aspects of customer communication, primarily because it is cheaper, and more convenient and **appear**s faster to users. While e-mail may resemble "written communication (paper), it doesn't work the same way, and effective communication via e-mail, particularly with angry or upset customers requires taking into account the unique characteristics of e-mail as a communication medium.

You are probably familiar with basic e-mail etiquette and practices like proper quoting in replies, not using all capital letters, and so on, so we will focus on the more important characteristics of e-mail that can cause problems with your customers.

THE RELIABILITY ISSUE

When you write a letter you don't think much about the reliability of the mail system or worry whether the customer/recipient will actually receive it. It's something we take for granted, although perhaps we should give it a bit more thought.

Snapshot

E-Mail Reliability?
Now that we are used to using e-mail, there's a tendency to take for granted it's reliability. Unfortunately, when you factor in spam filters, technical errors, and user errors, what you find is that while e-mail is pretty good for "getting there", it's far from perfect. Many a problem has come from e-mail that never arrived.

Similarly, with e-mail we make the assumption that an e-mail sent to a client is going to be received and read. Unfortunately, e-mail is not nearly as reliable as most people think and that can cause problems with customers. In fact, e-mail is sufficiently unreliable that it is not accepted as a formal way to provide important information or legal documents. It is primarily used to respond to customer queries. Yet, we forget that its imperfect.

When a customer corresponds with a company about an issue, or just asks a question, a number of things can happen, and only ONE of them is good. We hope the customer both receives and fully reads what is sent, and understands the contents of the message as you intended. That's the good part. Here are the bad possibilities, all of which represent ways the communication can "go bad".

Message gets:

• lost in YOUR e-mail server

• sent but gets lost in the Internet on way to recipient

• to recipient's mail server but server crash results in loss

- to mail server but account no longer exists (mail bounces - you may or may not get notified)

- to mail server but is deleted because it is mistaken as junk mail (spam)

- to mail server but is deleted because your entire domain is blocked (this is common due to forged e-mails)

- to software set up to "authenticate" you, but you never receive notification.

- to recipient mail box but person doesn't check the account anymore.

- to recipient mail box but is never seen because mail client deletes it or sends it to the junk mail folder)

- to recipient but it's missed among a mass of other mail.

- to recipient but person doesn't read it completely.

Daunting isn't it? It would be great if we knew exactly what percentage of e-mail goes awry, but it's hard to assess this because of the use of anti-spam software. The available numbers, while perhaps not definitive, are worrisome. In 2004, a study of major ISP's (Internet service providers), suggested that as much as 25% of REQUESTED corporate e-mail was inaccurately identified as junk mail and sent to the junk folder or deleted.[1]

How do we cope with an unreliable mail system, then, when there is strong pressure to provide help and services to customers through e-mail. Here are some ideas to prevent e-mail problems that can cause customer anger) and techniques to use when the customer claims to have never received the e-mail.

TACTIC 71: MODIFY YOUR E-MAIL MINDSET

Get out of the habit of assuming e-mail you send and e-mail customers send to you always arrives properly. If you don't address this you are going to make mistakes and have to wade through misunderstandings and problems that are unnecessary. Do not assume. When involved in an email discussion with a customer, and it appears you are at cross-purposes, the FIRST question to ask is *"Let's make sure we've been receiving each other's emails, OK?"*

TACTIC 72: USE AN E-MAIL DISCLAIMER NOTICE

Organizations often tag onto the end of an e-mail some disclaimer or notice about confidentiality, and while that may be a good idea, it's far less useful than having a single disclaimer that explains that e-mail tends to be unreliable and if no e-mail response is received within x days, to follow up using a specified phone number. Not only should such a disclaimer be on each e-mail, but it should be on every website, blog, or other online presence, beside the list of e-mail contacts.

We cannot control the reliability of e-mail, but by being in-formed, and by informing customers, we can prevent prob-lems and anger when e-mail goes awry. Better to have a cus-tomer understand the reason he has not received a response is due to lost -mail rather than employee dis-interest.

TACTIC 73: USE E-MAIL FOLLOW-UPS

CAUTION!

Follow-up On E-mail or Get Burned
Don't assume important e-mail will arrive. If an e-mail has important con-tent for the customer or for you, make a note to yourself to follow-up in a day or two to ensure it arrived, and the meaning was clear.

When you send an e-mail, if you do not receive a response when one might be expected, follow up with another e-mail to investigate. Simply say that you responded to the person's request on [date] and that you want to make sure your e-mail reply was received. Not only is this a good way to prevent misunderstandings, but it's a knock the socks off customer service practice that impresses clients and customers.

That said, it doesn't completely get around the e-mail reliability issue, and it does require you to track outgoing e-mails, or use some sort of reminder/bring forward system. Do it if it's possible.

TACTIC 74: USE OTHER FOLLOW-UP METHODS

Obviously following up on an e-mail with another e-mail isn't always going to work, so if the con-versation is "important", you may want to follow up with a phone call, provided the individual has already provided his or her number. As with the e-mail follow up this is impressive customer ser-vice. Now that Facebook, Twitter and LinkedIn are so popular you could also try contacting a cus-tomer on one of those, using the search function to find their login name(s).

Keep in mind that some people are very concerned about privacy issues and will wonder how you got their phone number (if they hadn't provided it) or their Facebook or Twitter identities. Some may be deeply offended by a contact that has not bee previously authorized, so for this reason con-sider whether contacting the customer via an alternative medium without permission is absolutely necessary. Also there may be circumstances where the alternative medium (e.g. phone) is less pri-vate and confidential, and the customer may not want anyone else to know he is using your ser-vices or buying products from you.

E-MAIL: NOT CONVERSATION, BUT NOT LETTER COMMUNICATION

E-mail is a deceptive medium because it appears to share characteristics of a real time conversation, since the interchanges can be so fast. It also appears to share the characteristics of letter communi-cation. In fact, it **incorporates the worst aspects** of both, requiring great care in communication. It's a very unique medium.

Below are some e-mail characteristics and some tactics to counter-balance the challenges of commu-nicating with angry customers via e-mail.

CAUTION!

Avoid Complex E-mails
People do not read e-mails carefully— nowhere near the way they might read/re-read a letter on paper. Guaranteed if you have five complex points to make in an email, the recipient will miss at least two, and get another one or two wrong.

◆ E-mail is an impulsive medium compared to letter writing. It's "impulsive" because people write off the tops of their heads, and hit the send button, often NOT reading before sending.

◆ As with the telephone (only worse), people say things in e-mail that are not considered or reflected upon. Hence, it's hard to judge the degree of upset from the tone of an e-mail, and it is easy to send an e-mail that conveys the wrong meaning or is easy to misinterpret. Many a person has wanted to "recall" an e-mail sent while angry, and some have even lost their jobs as a result of an impulsive e-mail!

◆ People often do not read e-mails in their entirety, as is also the case with anything that appears on their computer screens. Comprehension of your message(s) may be low, contributing to difficulties in resolving customer concerns. When you ask questions in e-mail, its often the case that you don't receive an answer (see tactic 77).

TACTIC 75: TREAT E-MAIL AS THE IMPULSIVE MEDIUM IT IS AND IGNORE THE BAIT.

Some people like to write irate e-mails, just like some people like to call on the phone to complain, even though they don't expect anything to change. E-mails are so easy to send that you can collect chronic e-mail senders just as you might collect chronic phone callers. In any event, treat the e-mail content as you would any bait. Ignore it, and if there is an issue that needs to be dealt with, refocus back to the problem. However, be sure to take note of the next tactic.

TACTIC 76: MOVE AWAY FROM E-MAIL FOR EMOTIONAL CONTENT

E-mail gives users a false sense of emotional connection, but as with any words (on a page or a screen), communicating emotion and/or within emotional situations is difficult using non face-2-face media. For this reason, it's best to rely on e-mail more for the communication of facts, places, times, meeting confirmations, etc., than for the offering of emotional support or addressing emotionally charged issues.

Be prepared to contact the e-mailer by phone (it's better than e-mail although not as effective as face-2-face for emotionally charged situations).

TACTIC 77: BE PREPARED FOR LACK OF COMPREHENSION AND STRUCTURE FOR COMPREHENSION

Most people assume that reading an e-mail or something on a computer screen is the "same" as reading a book or a letter. It's not. Eye scans (the pattern the eyes take) when reading a screen are different than on paper, and reading from a screen results in significantly less understanding of the content than does reading from paper, all things being equal.

This means that if when you communicate via e-mail, you will almost certainly come across rather baffling interpretations of what you have written., Recipients tend to scan, and fill in details from their own heads, rather than read each word. This also probably applies to you when YOU read e-mail.

E-mail is a poor medium for helping someone UNDERSTAND complex things, although it is a good medium for summarizing complex things as a follow up to face-to-face or telephone conversations.

Always be alert to the possibilities of misreading, or partial reading on your part and by others. When you send e-mail always re-read it before sending it, and try reading it from the perspective of the recipient. Read every word. In addition, structure the e-mail into short, single topic paragraphs. Use headings when possible. **Any paragraph that is longer than five or six lines is too long.**

When reading incoming mail, slow down. Also read every word BEFORE replying, and before replying **READ the entire message**. This will save time. Often, when you read the full message, you'll find your first responses are inaccurate or require editing.

When you draft your e-mail reply ALWAYS use the equivalent of active listening -- summarize your understanding of what the individual said. Request verification that you have understood..

Social Media and Communicating With Customers

It's time to turn to the use of more recent, and perhaps less familiar technology based communication media -- social media.

In 2008-2010, as a result of a number of factors, including mainstream publicity from television celebrities such as Ellen DeGeneres and Oprah, the public "discovered" social media and flocked to sign up to services such as Twitter, Facebook and LinkedIn, to name just of few of the most popular. The unifying idea behind all "social media" places is that people can interact and share information, messages, videos, pictures, etc with relative ease. The term encompasses blogs, video sharing sites such as YouTube, picture sharing sites, chat rooms -- in fact any online context that involves the ability to communicate from many people TO many people or from one person TO many people..

 Wise Thoughts To Ponder

Social Media—Overhyped
It's not that social media is irrelevant to customers and service. However, there are outrageous claims made abut it by people who clearly have agendas and will benefit from its use. This includes major research and consulting companies. When it comes to where things will end up with social media combined with customer service, NOBODY really knows, and if people claim to know, they are flat out lying. As of 2011, we lack the proper data and analysis to be able to understand what's going on now, let alone predict the future.

Wise Thoughts To Ponder

Thought Experiment
How bad IS Twitter for having meaningful conversations with customers? Try this. Set aside 30 minutes, and you and a colleague agree to discuss work issues but to never use more than eleven words per turn. If you actually last the 30 minutes drop me a line. I won't believe you, but drop me a line anyway.

Platforms for such sharing have existed for a very long time -- in fact even prior to wide spread access to the Internet, but the capability a) was not available to the masses; b) required a level of technical expertise most people lacked; and c) required hardware not common at the time. Now, with technology in many homes, schools and cafes, mass access is possible. People have indeed flocked to these services, at least to try them out, but don't be fooled by the numbers. For any social media platform, more people have obtained accounts and abandoned them than have obtained accounts and used them. Just a caution.

Organizations, seeing the raw numbers, jumped in because they felt the need to "get with it" and communicate with customers where the customers gather -- social media and networking sites. It is true that more and more customers look to Facebook and Twitter to see if they can communicate with companies there if they have issues with services or products. It is also the case that most customers, at least at this time, prefer to converse with companies via phone, provided phone support doesn't require the patience of Job. To put the issue in perspective there is research to suggest that only about 9% of Twitter users use it to obtain customer service. Given all the buzz, you would think it's way higher, but it's not.

The term social media covers so much ground it's hard to generalize, so we are going to deal with two of the sub-media -- short form communication (e.g. microblogging) and longer form communication (e.g. blogging, support forums).

SHORT FORM SOCIAL MEDIA (TWITTER, STATUS UPDATES ON FACEBOOK, LINKEDIN)

Short form social media platforms limit the number of characters that can be included in any single message. Twitter is probably the best known short form platform since its reason to exist involves the dissemination of 140 character (maximum length) "tweets". Its apparent growth has been huge but is an illusion due to the number of dead accounts and the number of people who don't ever send anything. In fact research also suggests that most tweets (> 90%) do not receive any acknowledgement, are not replied to and appear to slip into the ether unnoticed.

Both Facebook and LinkedIn (two more social media platforms) have added the ability to send short updates/statuses.

Twitter's reach is much smaller than most believe, but be that as it may, companies have jumped in to use Twitter as a means of communicating with customers, protecting their reputations, and yes, dealing with complaints online. It may turn out that jumping in without data to support the usefulness of doing so, will turn out to be a bad choice for companies, but at this point, we don't know.

Messages you send (tweets, updates) have very short shelf lives since they "stream" through accounts rather than sit IN accounts like e-mail does. That means that if you send information to your "friends" or "followers" who you think will read the message, many— perhaps most, **will not** see it. They may find it later if they search, but a significant number will not. People who are fanatical about reading anything YOU post are most likely to see most of what you post, but the average user/follower will not.

This is a HUGE and often ignored characteristic of short form social media that has both positive and negative implications for customer service. We'll get to that in a moment.

Twitter is a "venting" medium, where people are far more likely to tell others about their BAD experiences with this department or that store, than share their GOOD experiences. Or is it? That's just plain common sense, right? Well, no. It turns out that research has shown that most "mentions" of brands and companies tend to be neutral, and not negative, according to research that looks at Twitter and that among tweets that are exhibit some "sentiment" about a brand, positive comments are as common, or more common than negative ones.

Still, it's reasonable for any organization to be concerned about complaints, false information, rumors and even lies that might be spread on Twitter or on any other social media platform.

Contrary to what many "social media experts" say, it is simply not possible to counter complaints made in social media short forms by participating in those short forms. If you make people mad, they will tell at least "some" other people, and once the "genie is out of the box" the damage cannot be undone.

Why? It goes back to the transitory nature of tweets and short form social media communication. Managing reputation on Twitter is not an effective use of resources, because you cannot possibly communicate with even a small number of the people who saw the initial complaint or lie. You don't know who might have read a complaint. You can't target them to explain your position or clarify. And, you probably aren't going to change their perceptions of you even if you could do those things.

The GOOD news is that for the most part a person tweeting something negative about you is going to have almost NO visibility. That is their "reach" is tiny. Even if they appear to have an audience of, let's say 1,000 people, very few will actually read any one tweet, and of those, almost none will be relevant to you and your location.

Even in situations where people have tried to carry out a vendetta or complaint "program" against a particular company, the impact had been minimal, even when they set up accounts specifically to attack a particular company or air their complaints about a company. Single, unorganized customers have no more power now that before.

What about all the famous cases of customers fighting back? There actually are a few instances where someone has, almost entirely by chance, had a complaint aired on social media, "picked up" via traditional media (newspapers, TV, radio) etc. This happens so rarely that a company that spends time and resources to counteract a fluke event is foolish indeed. It's about as sensible as preparing for a snow storm, when you live in Barbados. It makes far more sense for a company to make sure it doesn't "screw up" in the first place.

If it sounds like Twitter is rather limited for use as a two way communication tool between customer and company, it is. And it isn't. It is helpful for finding people who need help or have complaints that might fall in your bailiwick. It's not useful for altering your reputation except to the extent that other people send good things out about you. It's an uncontrollable medium. So, how can you use it? Here are some relevant tactics for using short form social media.

Tactic 78: Use Twitter (short form) to send information - adjunct to other methods

Since the actual receive/read rate for Tweets is probably much lower than even e-mail, it's not a reliable form of information dissemination, but it can still be valuable for updates that do not require great detail such as traffic or road conditions for a particular area. Therefore use Twitter **in addition** to existing ways of getting information out there to customers. Note: Isn't it interesting that technology doesn't tend to replace earlier ways of doing things, but adds an EXTRA thing to do?). Make it clear to customers that Twitter is just one of the ways they can stay informed, and that it is imperfect. Use it to get people to signup for something you control (i.e. a newsletter).

Tactic 79: Monitor Twitter for Discussions of Your "domain"/Company

Pundits base the "need for monitoring" on the false belief that it's possible to fix a reputation once it has been damaged in social media. However there are other, better reasons to monitor what your customers, and potential customers, are saying. It's good for collecting information and getting a sense of what SOME of your customers are saying about you, and might provide ideas about future products and features that customers would like. That's valuable.

Tactic 80: Respond to Negative Tweets once in public, then shift to e-mail/phone

If you come across someone having a problem with your business, first respond to the negative tweet in public. You can use pretty standard phrasing but mix it up a bit. For example: *"Sorry you are having a problem". I work [here}. Can I help via e-mail?*

If you get a response, ask for an e-mail address or other method of contact. Twitter, is a poor medium for problem-solving, but also, there are issues of confidentiality and privacy. You also want to remove the "virtual audience" from the process. Any audience brings strange and distracting dynamics into a conversation, particularly if the customer is angry and upset.

TACTIC 81: ALWAYS ASK PERSON/CUSTOMER FOR PERMISSION TO CONTACT IN E-MAIL/PHONE

In some situations, you may have an e-mail address or phone number for someone without the person giving it to you in the online conversation. You might recognize a person who you have dealt with before, and in wanting to help, you e-mail or phone her. Bad idea. Always ask the customer to choose the form of contact when the INITIAL contact has been through an online process, such as Twitter or Facebook.

Large organizations, in particular, are seen by many as having too much information (the Big Brother thing), so never flaunt the contact information you have unless it's an emergency (such as suicide attempt possibility). If you surprise a customer by using a different medium, it's likely he will lash out, even if your intent is good.

 CAUTION!

Half-Hearted Social Media?
Half-Hearted efforts on social media are probably going to backfire. You need to commit enough resources to ensure you can respond to customers quickly and effectively on social media, or you just make things worse.

TACTIC 82: WRITE SIMPLE, ONE TOPIC SHORT FORM MESSAGES

It is incredibly easy for misunderstanding to occur in short form messages due to characters limitations. That's another reason to switch away from interacting on places like Twitter when dealing with a customer or customers. It's also important to make sure you "tweet" only one idea/topic per short message, avoid abbreviations if possible, and take time to craft that one topic. Express the idea simply.

Tweeting and other short forms of communication may look easy, but in fact, they are much harder to write than other longer forms.

Longer Form Communication Via Internet (Social Media, Blogs, Websites)

Longer form communication with customers refers to messaging formats that are not limited to a specific number of characters. Blogs, websites, support forums and discussion lists all fit in this category, whether the venue belongs to you/your company, or whether the venue is run and controlled by an independent third party. It's important to distinguish between what you control and what independent parties control, since obviously what you do and even the decision to be involved depends on how and who controls the forum, mailing list, etc.

Snapshot

Always Review Before You Send
When you use social media for business purposes, always re-read what you send prior to sending to make sure it is consistent— both in content and tone — with the reasons you are active on social media. Social media is quite informal and its easy to forget one's purpose.

In keeping with our theme about helping you deal with disgruntled customers, we'll focus on the how to deal with negative comments in public venues on the Internet.

Before we do that, though, here's your first tip: Assume that what you write on the Internet or Intranet WILL become public and will be there forever. **That applies to private emails** you might send to customers, too. Remember that even if you delete something from your blog, it's still "available" in countless other places. Consider what you write on the 'net to be forever.

There are also no "rules of fair play" when it comes to what gets posted online, or at least while there are rules there's no way to enforce fair play, so get used to the idea that people may "share" private communication, identify you personally, and spread false and inaccurate information about you and your company.

One more thing, before we look at strategies and tactics to deal with upset customers via "longer form" Internet communication. This applies to the content and formatting of any longer material you or you company posts to the Internet, whether its on your website, your own blog, someone else's blog, or in a support forum.

You must still conform to general rules and practices of good writing that apply to both paper and electronic media. In addition to those general rules. there are characteristics of the electronic medium that you should be aware of, since if you ignore them, you may end up creating misunderstanding with your customers, thus contributing to hostile behavior.

TACTIC 83: ATTEND TO THE LAYOUT OF YOUR ARTICLES, POSTS, COMMENTS AND ANSWERS, NOT JUST THE CONTENT

Since people scan computer monitors differently than they scan printed matter, it's important to have your key points stand out, so viewers will see them quickly, and pay attention. A lot of misunderstandings, and thus angry customers, happen because the text on websites or blogs is not written or formatted to take into account that viewers skim, and miss details. More effective layouts involve:

- Short paragraphs, with double spacing between each paragraph. Six to ten lines per paragraph is good although it depends on the screen width of your readers.

- Short sentences and simple sentence structures. Complex structures will be even more confusing online than on the printed page.

- Proper headings. Assume your reader is going to take a quick look at the page overall to see if what he is looking for can be found in the headings.

- The gist of the page should be readable without scrolling down the page. That doesn't mean that everything that is important needs to be stuffed at the top, but it does mean visitors should be able to quickly see what is on the rest of the page by looking at the top. Summaries in bold are good.

CAUTION!

Control? Use A Light Touch
Overuse of control and power on forums, discussion lists and blogs will almost always backfire. Use control to create a useful, pleasant environment where customers can communicate with each other and with you. Do not use control to squelch criticism aimed at you or your company.

TACTIC 84: STICK TO SIMPLE CONTENT WRITTEN IN STYLE SUITED TO YOUR DESIRED AUDIENCE, AND REVIEW BEFORE POSTING

Consistent with using a layout that promotes ease of reading and comprehension, use a writing style consistent with the way your target audience communicates. That doesn't mean ignoring rules of grammar just because your audience is younger, but it does mean you might tailor your messages differently if you are commenting on a blog site for lawyers compared with one for skateboarders. Use appropriate terminology but remember that online communication, with very few exceptions, is informal and should feel more like a conversation at dinner, than like a professional journal article.

Not only do you write to inform but you write to provide some flavor about who you are as a person. Personality counts, not only for marketing online, but also in establishing a persona/reputation that will shield you from online abuse.

To reiterate, keep things simple, and always review carefully what you've written before you send the post to the forum, list or blog. Review for typos, spelling, accuracy and above all, for tone.

Interacting On Venues You Don't Control

The areas your company provides to customers— a bulletin board type forum, or an interactive mailing list, or even a blog, are not the only places online where you and your company may be discussed. There are hundreds of thousands of forums and discussion areas on all kinds of topics, and they've been around since the availability of the Internet to the public. That's a very long time. Most are public and can be found via search engine, while some are private and hard to find.

For example, there are forums to discuss webhosting companies, cell phone providers, restaurants and hotels, and almost any popular product out there. There are even forums and discussion areas dedicated to a particular company, though these tend to be limited to the giants of industry such as Google, or Comcast.

RELEVANCE TO YOUR BUSINESS?

What is the relevance to your business? How do these forums get used by people unhappy about your company, and what can you do about them? All good questions, and deserving of a book dedicated to answering them. We'll have to limit ourselves somewhat with our answers, but here's the gist.

Not only will customers complain on YOUR Internet forums, blogs and discussions, but they may also do so on venues that are privately owned. These other sites are apart from major sites like Facebook, Twitter, or the few industry related "review sites".

Is this a concern for you and your company? That's a call you have to make, and it will depend on the popularity and level of influence a particular site may have and how much time you want to spend replying online. For example, "TripAdvisor" is a fairly popular site where people post reviews of hotels. It's well known and it is used by people trying to find hotels. People pay some attention to the comments there. If you come across negative comments about your hotel on TripAdvisor, it's probably a good idea to respond (see later tactics). If you come across similar comments on a blog nobody goes to, and that doesn't show up high in search rankings for keywords that apply to your business, it may not be worthwhile taking the time to response. You make that call. It's always good to respond to reasonable, rational reviews and comments about your business. It's not always a good thing to respond to rants from unreasonable people online.

Here's a strong positive for participating in some of these interactive areas that has to do with PREVENTION of problems. When you participate and help others on third party forums, you will build credibility and trust and that is a huge plus when and if an unreasonable customer attacks yo online. Others will defend you provided you have created a positive "vibe".

Now, that said, how do you respond to negative comments on venues over which you have no control? Let's pull a list of principles and tactics together and list them:

TACTIC 85: HOW TO RESPOND TO NEGATIVE COMMENTS ON ONLINE VENUES OVER WHICH YOU HAVE NO CONTROL

1. Almost all of the principles and tactics we've presented so far apply to how you interact with dissatisfied customers online, so use them. The CARP system works online, but you should place additional emphasis on acknowledging, refocusing and problem-solving. Don't dodge tough RELEVANT questions, but quickly refocus.

2. Decide whether a particular comment deserves a response. If you see a blog comments like "Bozo's Auto Body sucks", should you bother? Probably not because you aren't likely to have a reasonable conversation that portrays you in a positive light. If the comments are intelligent and rational, then a response could be in order.

3. Remember that "what you focus on, you get more of". Acknowledge, Refocus on the present and future, and problem-solve. It's not about blame.

4. Don't defend our counter-attack. You may "explain" by providing some basic facts in a very few sentences, but lengthy explanations defending why your business does things a certain way are not likely to impress people.

5. Remember for every participant in a discussion online there are many more observers watching in silence. Don't let that worry you though. The influence of most forums and discussion lists tends to be small — much smaller than we are lead to believe.

6. Triage. That means, choose your battles. Some comments are not worth dignifying, and others are. Consider popularity of the venue, whether well known people are involved in the comments, the credibility of the venue operators, how much time you have to devote to interacting with people there and any other factors that come to mind. Remember you run/are employed by a business, probably with limited resources, and you have to decide how to allocate time for business purposes. **Just because a comment might be offensive or make you angry does NOT mean it deserves a response.**

7. When you respond, identify yourself as a representative from your company. It's always good to include your position/company name at the bottom of any posts you send on behalf of the company.

8. Offer to deal with the complaining customer offline, preferably on the phone, or email is a good choice too. The reason is you want to remove the audience factor from the initial complaint, and if it's a busy discussion area, you are going to receive a lot of comments from the peanut gallery that can overwhelm you and obscure the conversation. Make the offer publicly on the forum along with indicating that you'd be willing to post a summary of how the issue was resolved to the public forum.

9. Follow-up publicly when possible with both the customer and the forum members after resolution.

10. Finally, if you visit the most important and relevant online discussion areas related to your company, and post occasionally, your presence will usually be welcomed, and you will gain "credibility and 'good guy' points" for participating. These points can be drawn upon when and if complaints occur.

Tactic 86: What NOT To Do When Responding To Negative Comments on Venues You Do Not Control

Here's some things you should avoid, once again, in point form.

1. Don't act like you own the joint. Seriously. You are a guest on any forum that does not belong to you or your company, so get acquainted with THEIR rules and procedures. Most serious forums and discussion areas have people, called moderators, whose job it is to do minor policing.

2. Even if you are extremely offended by the content of a forum post or blog comment, pause, consider and think before responding either publicly or privately to a moderator. If you think the comment is libelous, BEFORE you rush off in all directions spouting fire, forward the comment to a manager or legal counsel to determine whether there is any legal course of action. Usually there isn't, or that course of action will do more to damage your business' credibility than would simply ignoring the message.

3. Don't take a threatening tone with either the comment poster, or the owners/moderators of the discussion area. If you do that, even in "private", your "threats" are likely to be spread publicly making you look either very nasty and unpleasant, or very stupid. Unfair comments can cause you to want to strike back and punish, but life isn't always fair. Don't act stupidly and from a place of high emotion. However, you can use some assertive limit setting and spell out consequences if **absolutely** necessary.

4. If you see a comment on a blog, or forum that is completely and utterly inappropriate, you can report the post to the moderator and ask that it be removed, or that the moderator "take appropriate action". Limit your request to removal of the post, rather than "demanding" the offending part be banned. Don't rant. Don't rave. Be nice. If you've been participating in the forum before, you'll get more positive results.

5. Don't be a nasty customer when you respond to another nasty customer on someone else's blog. Nuff said?

Now, The Exceptions

As you read the points in the last two tactics, their value is probably self-evident. The actions and "don't do's" are conservative in nature, and they apply to most people in most businesses. There are, however, some circumstances when you might want to go another route, one that's more risky. It's a route that I've taken, it's one less travelled, but it might be good to understand it, in case it applies to you.

In my business, I am both the product and the service. I don't market per se. I see myself in the learning business, and my

 Wise Thoughts To Ponder

Personas

Whether we do so intentionally or not we all present ourselves, or part of ourselves, to others online via a persona. That just means we want to come across in a certain way that fits how we want people to see us. We all have multiple personas we present to the world. Since this happens anyway, doesn't it make sense to think about how we represent ourselves to others online, and make sure that that representation is in our interests?

company (and myself) produce materials/books distributed world wide to help people learn about business and interpersonal relationships. I do things my way. In fact that's one of the main reasons I quit my regular job almost twenty years ago to start my own business. I wanted to do "it" my way.

I want people to see me (and hire me) on the basis of how my thinking, which tends to be contrarian in nature, can help their businesses or in some cases their personal lives. I want people to read my books because they expect something a little different — a different perspective. I want to differentiate between my company and any possible competitors on the basis that only one company has...well...me. This may sound arrogant, but it's not. I'm not the best thing since sliced bread. I'm hardly even melba toast. It's just how I want to do things.

Snapshot

Never Rude
You can fire a customer. You can refuse service. However, if you care about how any prospective customers might see you, then you must never be rude to existing customers. It's kind of obvious. Are there exceptions to this rule? No. Not really.

My approach is: *"Hey, here I am. What you see is what you get* (albeit a bit more polite in person)."

How does this lead into exceptions? First I don't worry about negative comments online. I'm not going to stop "shooting off my mouth" because of negative comments. I would rather be seen as a "good thinker", than a "nice person, although, in person, I am often both.

Often, on social media sites, I don't bother responding, because there simply isn't any point. People who like the bluntness, and yes, even more aggressive style I use online will continue to appreciate it, and those that don't won't. Frankly, if people want me to be "different", they aren't my customers anyway.

My online persona, which is gruff, curmudgeonly and sometimes even rude (by the standards of others) is consistent with how I want to be seen — **as an independent critical thinker who is going to provide his opinion truthfully and openly.**

All this is to say that my approach to online discussion, including negative comments is **consistent with my business strategy,** and both my personal and business needs. I have often disregarded what I "preach" in this book ONLINE, because I have a reason to do so. I may not always share the reason for being blunt or rude, but there is almost always a thought out reason. If someone takes the time to get to know me, I'm usually willing to explain the reasoning.

Two questions remain. First, have I lost business as a result of being loud and "in yer face" on issues online? No doubt. Would I change anything I've done in terms of communicating on the Internet? Particularly with non-customers? Nope. My success has been financially overwhelming and my online persona has attracted book publishing contracts I never would have received otherwise, to name one benefit.

Second, do I advise others to do things the way I do them? Nope.

One more thing about this. While I am aggressive in posting comments on blogs, I am ALWAYS pleasant, supportive and helpful to my customers if they have problems or issues.

Tactic 86: Monitoring For Mentions of You/Company

Obviously, if you don't know about angry customers, you can't try to counteract any negative impact they might have as a result of their comments on the boards and discussion areas you are unaware of. It should be standard practice to search around for mentions of your company, and/or your name, if it's associated with the business. It's not that difficult.

Use **Bing or Google** search engines to search for relevant key terms, and while you are at it, you might want to search for comments about your competitors. For example, if you run a restaurant, search for restaurant name review. Learn to use search engines efficiently. That's a good investment of time. Not only will you find comments about your own business, but you can learn about what prospective customers are interested in (collecting business intelligence) and what your competitors are doing. You will also find forums and discussion areas about topics related to your business where you should have an ongoing "presence" as a representative of your business. Some forums can be very influential.

You may also want to do separate searches on the big three (or four if you count YouTube) social media sites — Twitter, LinkedIn, Facebook, YouTube). Generally their contents would be included in Bing and Google search results anyway, but a quick search doesn't cost you anything but a minute or two.

On Google, you can set up ongoing searches that run automatically, with new results being sent to your email box, which is a great feature.

Blogs and Forums You Control—Dealing With Complaints

Dealing with customer comments and complaints on your company blog or forum, or elsewhere where you control who can post, what gets posted and whether posts stay published, is not all that different from how you deal with complaints anywhere. For that reason, we'll focus on the differences having to do with having control.

If you don't know, when you own/run a blog, support forum, or discussion area, you can set it up to be very laissez-faire (hands-off) or you can set it up so you exert maximum, and even total control over what visitors see and what gets posted. Most common for company blogs and comment areas is to moderate posts — that is, each post requires explicit approval before it is available to the public.

The prime reason it's done that way is NOT to filter out unfavourable comments as much as it is aimed at improving the experience of visitors — eliminating spam and other junk posts. Nothing speaks badly about a company more than having an official discussion area that is filled with swearing and childish behavior. It DOES reflect on the owner. Here are some pointers directly related to dealing with complaints on your own blogs and forums and some tips indirectly related to the topic.

TACTIC 87: DEALING WITH COMPLAINTS IN DISCUSSIONS YOU CONTROL

As with some of the other tactics in this chapter, we'll present principles and suggestions about how to deal with complaints on social media sites you own/control. Obviously the major difference between having and not having control is that you can attempt to stop or delete posts and messages you deem inappropriate.

1. Have a clearly available policy that includes what is permissible and not permissible on the forum/blog, how the content is moderated, and the conditions under which posts may be refused and deleted. In addition, it's good to explain what basis you might use to ban users. Keep in mind that as in all things, the best use of power involves not using it unless absolutely necessary.

2. Apply the policy fairly, equitably and consistently, as best you can. If you are responsible for running the public area, once in a while check with colleagues or others to examine any decisions you have made about removing or preventing posts from becoming public.

3. When responding to complaints, as with any public forums, don't be aggressive or defensive. Explanations (keep them short) for company actions are OK, but keep them factual. Make use of your full arsenal of defusing tools.

4. Always acknowledge the frustration of posters if they post complaints, but remember that while an acknowledgement is important, customers posting will expect an honest effort to solve the substantive problem.

5. Have a notice clearly displayed that indicates **how long a customer should expect to wait** for a response if and when he's posted on your blog, support area, or discussion group, and stick to it. Nothing is worse than no response, or a delayed response.

6. In forums and blogs, once a thread or issue has been resolved, or is "past its freshness date" at minimum, close the discussion. That involves setting the software so it doesn't allow additional comments. It's pointless to have discussions around problems that have already been resolved, or complaints from long ago. However, make sure the resolution has been clearly noted in the thread, preferably in the last post in the thread.

7. Remember that people are watching, and if they don't like your responses and behavior, they may extend the conversation to other venues where you have less control. That's not a terrible thing, but it's something the company can do without.

8. If you move attempts to resolve a problem from the public area to more private communication (email or phone), indicate that in the complaint thread, and don't forget to update the public thread once the issue has been dealt with, even if the outcome was not necessarily the one the customer wanted.

9. In situations where obscene language is used as part of complaints, post a response which welcomes the customer's input PROVIDED the obscenities are absent. Then you'll want to remove the message or at least the offending words.

10. Banning people from posting is simply a fact of life these days — a necessity in fact because of the spam that any public forum attracts. Try to be as transparent as possible by explaining the rules periodically. Banning people for filing complaints and expressing upset and frustration is not a good idea unless they violate other rules in your conduct policy. For example users who attack others in uncivil ways can be warned, and then banned. Similarly people who persist in using obscene language despite being warned can also be removed in the interests of all visitors.

11. Keep in mind that while you can ban people/accounts in your software, it's pretty easy for someone to get around that. That's why banning should only be reserved for severe violations of your community rules, such that the violations affect the enjoyment and usefulness of the forum/blog by their customers.

12. Finally, consider carefully how and when posts will be posted. There are various options available depending on your software. You can allow everyone to post unmoderated, right through requiring approval for all posts. The unfortunate reality is that most forums are plagued by spam, often sent automatically, and you MUST deal with that problem quickly, or users will simply not come back. If that means you have to moderate all posts, that's what you have to do.

Conclusions & Reminders

In many ways, companies are still exploring how social media can be best used for communication with customers. Just to reiterate, at this point, in 2011, we know remarkably little about how what is said and read on social media actually affects customer behavior in the "real world". Those who claim otherwise, and that includes so-called "research firms" in the space, are ignorant, sloppy, or have agendas unstated about products and services they might supply to address customer service via social media channels.

Footnotes:

[1] Reported at: http://itmanagement.earthweb.com/columns/executive_tech/article.php/3341991
Brian Livingston - Is One-Fourth of Your E-Mail Getting Lost?

Chapter XVII — Audiences, Groups, Crowds and Mobs

INTRODUCTION

Most of this book has focused on dealing one to one with the difficult customer, since the majority of employees work on that basis. However, you may find that as part of your job, you are expected to work with groups of people, perhaps making presentations of one sort or another. In the situation where groups may contain members who are hostile or highly resistant to your message, you need to be able to defuse within a group context.

Even if group work is not part of your job responsibilities, groups of two or three (as in a family) may be involved in run of the mill customer discussions. Having several people involved complicates the process.

There are two different but challenging situations that involve communicating to an audience. The first applies to all employees, while the second applies only to employees who give presentations or meet with groups. Both require finesse, grace and patience.

GROUP DYNAMICS CHANGE BEHAVIOR

Before we talk about these two contexts and what you can do to counter hostility, and "be heard", it's important to realize that people in a group (a group being more than one person) act differently as a result of being in a group, than if they were alone. The mere fact that a person is with another person who can hear and participate in a conversation with you changes things. It almost always makes it more difficult to communicate a difficult message, or work with a hostile person. It's also possible to use group dynamics to your benefit, so we'll cover that in the section on presentations.

ACCIDENTAL AND INCIDENTAL AUDIENCES

Let's deal with a situation that faces most workers who deal with customers. What happens when an angry person interacts and is in public view of other customers?

This occurs often. We call it the effect of **accidental audiences**, since the audience is there, not by intent of the angry customer or the employee, but is just "in attendance" for their own reasons.

How does this affect your decision making when dealing with an irate customer? One problem is that the addition of other strangers to the angry discussion can have unpredictable effects. For example, on one hand the hostile individual may be acting so badly that observers support you, either via their body language, or less commonly, through their own comments. On the other hand, the onlookers may share their own frustrations with your company, and try to pile on, joining the verbal attack. The latter creates a kind of group momentum and while the use of the term "mob" is a little over the top, the subsequent behavior of a group of angry frustrated people joining in can certainly have mob-like characteristics.

Although the effects of the accidental audience are somewhat unpredictable, we know that most of the outcomes are
not what you want, and often are not what the angry customer wants either. People who come for service generally
expect some modicum of privacy for their discussions, and
do not want to "perform" in front of a crowd. Usually. Then
there are the people who will PLAY to the crowd for support, real or imagined, but certainly hoped for, and enjoy
the attention and pressure involved.

Even if observers take your "side", that creates problems if
they vocalize, since it opens the door for disputes between
and among customers, and those can turn violent very quickly.

TACTIC 89: OBSERVE CUSTOMER FOR SIGNS OF PLAYING TO ACCIDENTAL AUDIENCE

If you deal with customers and members of the public in a public environment (e.g. a counter, or
where there is a waiting area), you can't serve every customer in private or out of earshot of the rest
of those waiting. For the most part you don't have to anyway. However, you may need to take control of a situation where the angry customer is playing to the audience while he or she is being unpleasant or abusive to you. When you see the signs that this is occurring then you need to make
every attempt to remove the audience, and/or isolate the customer. Here's what to look for:

- Occasional glancing at/back at the audience while she interacts with you.

- Raised voice in a way that suggests he wants everyone to hear what he has to say (the tone is
  different when the person wants an audience as opposed to just being angry).

- Obvious directing of comments to the audience (e.g. *"Hey, you're with me, right?"*

Be alert for these signs. When you see them, take action to remove the audience-customer contact. If
you don't, the interaction may go on much longer than otherwise, and you run the risk of encouraging the mob mentality.

TACTIC 90: CHECK THE BYSTANDER EMOTIONAL TEMPERATURE

Even if the hostile customer is NOT playing to the crowd, you need to monitor what they are doing, and their emotional states. Imagine that a customer comes in with what seems to be a reasonable request, but that for some bureaucratic reason, you are not permitted to give him what he
wants. It happens. You'd like to help. It makes sense to do it. You just can't. The customer gets angry and raises his voice, but isn't showing any desire to involve bystanders.

However, the audience, waiting with not much to do during the wait, watches and listens. How do you think this is going to affect how THEY behave once it's their turn to talk to you and your colleagues?

Of course, they are going to be affected by seeing "another corporate employee" act "heartlessly", and while many won't say anything, they will still be more likely to be hostile if their own conversations go badly. Some **will** say something, and it's not going to be pleasant

By checking on bystander emotional states you will have a better idea if you need to remove the audience from the equation and prepare yourself mentally for negative comments from those waiting.

Look for hostile body language, out of the ordinary tensing, whispering among the strangers. There will always be some of this. If you monitor, look for CHANGES. Of course, if the audience is making overt remarks to you, whether they be in support of you, or in support of the customer, it's probably time to change the venue of the primary interaction.

TACTIC 91: SMILE, THEY ARE WATCHING

It makes sense that you would prefer the bystanders be on your side, not on the side of the angry customer. In actuality you should prefer that they stay quiet and neutral so as not to increase the possibility of conflict and violence among customers.

Believe it or not, there are things you can do to keep bystanders neutral, or on your side. First, realize they ARE watching and listening, and specifically they are watching and listening to YOU and how you behave. They don't much care about the angry customer, except how his behavior affects them (longer wait), but they DO care about you. They will judge whether you are being fair, and professional.

One thing about most groups is that there is a tendency for group members to step in when they perceive one person being unfair and mean to another person. Out of line is the catchphrase. If you maintain your cool, act professionally and calmly in the face of provocation, people waiting will often congratulate you when it's their turns to talk to you. At minimum, they won't jump in to support the hostile person. Being likeable and reasonable provides some protection from mob-like behavior.

On the other hand, the best way to mobilize people in a group is to act unprofessionally, or in a cold, bureaucratic way. You lose any sympathy you might have had, and even if the "other guy" is worse, onlookers will take his side because you are the employee.

TACTIC 92: CONTROL THE WAITING AREA ATMOSPHERE THROUGH COMMUNICATION

This is a preventative step to try to reduce hostility generally, by connecting with waiting customers. Connecting with and communicating with onlookers is particularly important when there is a delay, perhaps as a result of a disruption from a single hostile customer or one who acts out. When possible connect with customers waiting through both eye contact and announcements to the waiting group. Indicate how long the wait is, on average, and any shortcuts they might take to accomplish their tasks without waiting in line further. Let them know what they will need when they get to the "window" to be served so they can speed up their visit. Remember that people don't like waiting but they absolutely HATE waiting when they lack enough information about why and how long the delays will be.

Snapshot

Those Who Wait
Let them know what they will need when they get to the "window" to be served so they can speed up their visit. Remember that people don't like waiting but they absolutely HATE waiting when they lack enough information about why and how long the delays will be.

Do all of this in a non-bureaucratic and friendly voice, not the voice of an army drill sergeant. Yes, you want to offer help to make things more efficient, but you are also creating an image. A positive image will help you when you deal with a customer who tries to play to that audience, if the audience already likes you and appreciates your effort.

Tactic 93; Remove The Audience Or The Customer

When possible, try to isolate the hostile individual from the audience. This may mean bringing the person out of the public area, or if you are in the field, it may involve some excuse for moving the client away from other people. For example if you are conducting an insurance claim inspection and talking to the client in front of his/her family or employees, you might say:

Mr. Smith, let's go over to the barn to see whether... "

In this case you are trying to move the client away from the rest of the family.

Some offices/companies have small conference rooms to which a customer can be relocated if the need arises for increased privacy, or for more isolation from the audience. This is an excellent idea that has proven to be very successful in calming people down by removing the audience factor.

If you cannot relocate, try to remove the audience effect by requesting that the person could lower his volume so others in the room won't hear his private details. Make the request so it appears you are protecting his interests, rather than your own. You can also use distraction techniques to try to shift his attention from the audience to a specific object, form or paper that is relevant.

Dealing With The Ally/Friend/Companion (Theirs)

There's another situation involving audiences that needs addressing. It's not uncommon to deal with a customer who is accompanied by a friend, family member or other companion. This may be because the actual client wants a witness to the interaction, or wants help in making decisions, or it may simply be that the individual brought her children along out of necessity. Most of the companion situations aren't problematic. Difficulties arise when the companions interfere with communication, or encourage the customer to behave angrily or inappropriately. Whatever the reasons for being there the presence of a companion changes the dynamics, again, often for the worse.

In angry situations with a companion, particularly a family member, it's possible to get some strange interfering dynamics. For example, in a husband and wife situation, the husband may be more aggressive than he would otherwise be without his wife present because he doesn't want an argument from his wife when he gets home. In the reverse, the companion may frequently jump in and answer questions you address to the actual customer. You really do not want to get caught between and betwixt husband and wife, or any other pair of family members.

How you handle these situation will depend on the context. You cope with a lawyer as companion differently than you would a child as companion. Here are a few tactics.

TACTIC 94: USE EYE CONTACT/BODY LANGUAGE TO FOCUS

Eye contact and body language are useful for maintaining control over a conversation because they signify/indicate with whom you are interacting, AND from whom you expect the response. When dealing with a companion that tends to interrupt or answer your questions when you need the customer to answer, do not make eye contact with the companion and keep your body orientation towards the customer. That means facing the customer, and leaning towards the customer.

Gestures can be used to "invite" the customer (and not the companion) to answer. For example, ask the question while making eye contact with and orienting your body towards the customer and away from the companion.

Snapshot

Friends and Relatives
Eye contact and body language are useful for maintaining control over a conversation because they signify/ indicate with whom you are interacting, AND from whom you expect the response. When dealing with a companion that tends to interrupt or answer your questions when you need the customer to answer, do not make eye contact with the companion and keep your body orientation towards the customer.

At the same time, hold your hand horizontally (parallel to the ground) , PALM UP towards the customer. The palm up position is an invitation to talk. If you are interrupted by the companion, you can glance briefly at the companion, hold your hand up in a "whoa" position (hand almost vertical, palm facing towards companion), then switch eye contact back to the customer.

These movements are consistent with our use of verbal self-defense techniques, in that they do not focus attention on the issue of who is talking.

There are exceptions to focusing on the customer.. If you are dealing with someone who is being accompanied because the customer herself is not completely able to communicate or understand (e.g. cannot speak English, elderly and/or has trouble communicating), then of course direct your attention to the companion, but make sure you attend to BOTH customer and companion. A common error is to completely ignore the customer and attend to the companion caretaker, and that's rude and infuriating.

TACTIC 95: REMOVE, SEPARATE, ISOLATE

The most effective tactic for dealing with a third party is to remove the third party, separate the people, and/or isolate the individuals from each other. That's not always possible, because you may not be afforded the physical space to allow that (i.e. two locations, at least one private), or the companion may need to be present to help, or may be permitted explicitly due to statutes or regulations (i.e. a lawyer accompanying a client to an inquiry).

The best approach, if the physical space allows, is to offer a plausible reason for separating that does not focus on your need or desire to keep the companion quiet or out of the picture. Subtle is usually best, particularly at first.

First OFFER the customer the option of speaking to you privately, away from the companion if the companion is not necessary for the discussion. For example, if you are at a front counter:

> *Mr. Smith, there's a lot of background noise here, so perhaps you can just come behind the counter so we can talk more privately. Mrs. Jones, if you would like to take a seat, I'm sure we can wrap this up in a minute or two.*

If there are objections choose either a stronger "invitation" and explanation, or give in and deal with both at the same time, depending on how badly the companion is interfering with the process.

You can do a similar thing on the phone if there are children in the background, or there is someone with the caller, and interrupting from the background. You can SUGGEST that the caller move to a quieter area, because you are having trouble hearing, and you want to make sure you understand the caller so you can help.

The key here is to frame your needs in terms of helping the customer.

TACTIC 96: USE A TEAM APPROACH

A team defusing approach may be helpful — where you speak to one party, and your colleague deals with the other. Ideally each "pair" is out of earshot of the other. This may or not be practical in your workplace, but if it is, it can be a powerful technique, not just for solving the companion problem, but also for dealing with a single client.

A team approach to defusing hostility can be more effective than only one person dealing with the situation. Team approaches are particularly effective in audience situations.

Because team defusing is so dependent on the individuals involved, we can't tell you how to go about it. Different individuals have different strengths and prefer different roles when working in a defusing team. Sit down with colleagues and figure out what might be effective in your work context.

Delivering Presentations To Resistant and Hostile Groups

If, as part of your job, you give presentations to groups of people, you need to be prepared to deal with resistance, and sometimes outright hostility and heckling. The frequency of these unpleasant events is often determined by the kinds of presentations you are called upon to give. If you often give bad news of one sort or another to groups of people, you will run into these things. If most of your presentations are sales type presentations not likely to make people upset, you may go a long time without coming across these. Nevertheless, it's good to be prepared, skill wise.

Let's look at some specific tactics directed specifically at prevention and defusing audience situations.

TACTIC 97: KNOW WHEN YOU ARE HEADED FOR TROUBLE OR BEING ATTACKED

When people do presentations and they are not professional public speakers, they often lose touch with the audience, and don't know what's going on in the group. As such it's possible that you may not notice that the level of resistance and anger in the group is growing, or that you are in fact under a kind of public attack. Heck, there are a lot of things to keep track of when one does a speech so it's not surprising. It's important to be observant of the group. Often you can predict what they will do, and who in the group will be problematic just by paying attention.

 Bet You Didn't Know

Hecklers Can Help With Credibility
If you are faced with hecklers or unreasonable behavior in groups, you have either an opportunity or a problem. Handle these situations well and your credibility will rocket skyward. Mess up how you handle these situations and you will turn off even the most reasonable audience members. Truth is, it's all part of the job.

Typically resistant groups exhibit some or many of the following behaviors:

- Resistant body language (signs of disinterest/anger)

- Leading and misleading questioning

- Interruptions

- Attempts to hold the floor

- Outright insults

- Side-tracking to other issues

Inexperienced presenters often react to these behaviors in ways that increase problems rather than decrease them. Consistent with our discussion of the abuse game it is IMPERATIVE that you **do not respond defensively or aggressively.**

TACTIC 98: FOCUS ON THE BEST POSSIBLE OUTCOME

Your best ally, and your worst enemy is yourself. If you focus on creating the best possible outcome, and prevent yourself from acting out of fear (defensiveness or aggression), things will work out. They probably aren't going to work out perfectly. There will always be some audience members who will leave angry or disappointed, but you simply are not going to please everyone. If you can't handle that reality, then you can't be an effective spokesperson, and probably even worse, the stress of disapproval will affect your health and welfare. As you gain more experience, you will realize that you will survive even the toughest situations, and may learn to see speaking to resistant groups as a challenge.

In addition remember "What you focus on you get more of". The more you focus on negative audience behaviors the more likely you will get exactly those behaviors

TACTIC 99: HAVE FAITH IN THE GROUP PROCESS AND IN HUMAN BEINGS.

Groups, even hostile ones, tend to have a sense of fair play. If attackers appear unreasonable, and you appear calm and reasonable, the group will mobilize to discourage the unfair attacks. It cuts both ways. If the group members feel you are evasive, defensive, over controlling, aggressive or arrogant, they will swarm you.

Don't over-react, and stay in control and you can rely on the goodness of human beings to help (at least a little, but sometimes a lot).

TACTIC 100: ENHANCE CREDIBILITY

Credibility is enhanced when you appear to present a balanced set of arguments, both in favor and against what you are advocating. Clearly the preponderance of the evidence should be on your side, but you must acknowledge weaknesses in your position. By bringing up the weaknesses, you pre-empt attacks.

Credibility is also enhanced when the audience perceives you as **somewhat similar to them**. Some factors that affect these perceptions include:

- clothing and demeanor

- level, type and complexity of language (the more similar to the way the audience talks the greater the appearance of similarity)

- demonstrated understanding of the implications of your content/ideas for the audience members

- whether you have "been there"

Credibility is enhanced when you make the concerns of the audience your major focus and concern, as opposed to <u>your</u> concerns or those of your organization.

TACTIC 101: PREPARE PROPERLY

In order to establish credibility, and reduce hostile behavior you must understand your audience beforehand. This means preparing properly. You need to know the following so you can address them before the audience does:

Snapshot

Pre-emptive Strike
Since you've done your homework and know enough about your audience to anticipate their concerns and objections to your message, what do you do with that information? You intentionally bring up their concerns early on and address them as best you can.

- concerns, fears, of the audience with respect to your content and company

- kinds of objections likely to be brought up

- any positive benefits for the audience connected with your ideas and presentation

- the audience's normal style of communicating (formal, informal, type of language use, academic, jargon use, etc), so that you can match that language.

Also as part of your preparation do the following:

- Anticipate objections, prepare your counter-position, so you can broach the objections and your position first.

- Prepare and provide a well thought out agenda that outlines the purpose, format and benefits of the presentation for the audience. Plan on including time for questions and comments, as part of the agenda. In situations where a person tries to sidetrack the gathering, you can refocus on the agenda (but you have to have one in the first place).

TACTIC 102: FOCUS ON THE CONCERNS OF YOUR AUDIENCE

Your credibility will be enhanced when you make the concerns of the audience your major focus, as opposed to YOUR concerns (company concerns). The audience will be more open if they feel you are there for them, and not as a mouthpiece expressing the party line. It's understandable that you will feel your job is to get across the points your company wants you to cover. If that is all you do you will be in big trouble. You must demonstrate to the audience that you understand their concerns. You do that in two different ways, explained in the next two tactics).

TACTIC 103: PREEMPTING OBJECTIONS AND "THEIR" ISSUES

Since you've done your homework and know enough about your audience to anticipate their concerns and objections to your message, what do you do with that information? You intentionally bring up their concerns early on and address them as best you can. It's much better for YOU to explain:

> "*I know what's probably going on in your head. You are concerned that the changes in the farm insurance plan are going to result in inadequate payouts on claims. Let me explain how this will work.*"

If they bring it up, you lose the initiative and if you bring it up it shows you understand them.

TACTIC 104: BALANCE, NOT PROPAGANDA

Pretty much everything has pro's and con's. That will be the case for whatever you are presenting to an audience. There's a mistaken notion that concentrating ONLY on the good points will be better than a balanced approach which admits to the "con's". That only sometimes works when you have a naive, uninformed audience, that won't catch on that you are not being open with them, and it's NEVER a good idea to assume that. If you present a balanced perspective, which, of course is slightly weighted towards the company position, you will be perceived as fair and open minded. That reduces attacks. Balanced presentations are also more credible.

TACTIC 105: TEAM UP

We've already talked about team defusing on a one-to-one level, but it also applies to presentations. If it is at all possible, present with a teammate. While presenting in tandem adds additional complexity to the process, since you need to have your signals straight, it provides some strong benefits.

First, there will always be someone there to "jump in" if the other gets befuddled, lost or stumped by a question. Second, there will always be one person "observing" and it's easier to read the temperature of a group when you can sit back and watch. The third reason to present with a partner is to allow each of you to specialize in a portion of the content, so as to lighten the load. This is particularly useful when your message is complex.

Finally, two presenters can mean two different viewpoints, and perspectives. For example, a team of one male and one female would be far superior to one or other only, when presenting on a topic like pay equity or sexual harassment in the workplace. The advantages to team presentations are simply huge, provided it is practical.

TACTIC 106: TECHNIQUES FOR SIDE-TRACKING, DIRECT INSULTS, HECKLING AND INTERRUPTIONS

Side-tracking issues and off-topic questions should be acknowledged. To refocus you can re-introduce the purpose of the session from the agenda, acknowledge that the person's concern is important to him, and offer to discuss it in another forum (coffee break, after main session, etc).

Do not focus on the sidetracking. If person persists, repeat your offer to discuss after meeting. Never argue. Repeat until person gives up. You can also focus attention on the formal agenda, and suggest time restrictions are such that you have get back to the next item.

Direct insults should be dealt with briefly. Start by acknowledging the emotion of the attacker (usually anger, or concern). Try this phrasing:

> *Clearly you feel strongly about this, and want to talk about it further. Let's discuss this at (name time/venue). How does that sound to you?* (note the cooperative question at the end)

Repeat this in calm tone, if necessary. Avoid taking any bait. Often people hurling insults simply want you to get upset.

Heckling and interruptions are handled differently depending on their persistence. Sometimes they can be ignored, sometimes you can stop talking until the person stops, and add a non-verbal hand sign for the person to stop. Sometimes you can ask the person to stop, while inviting discussion privately. Or you can ask the person to "hold" the question or comment until the pre-planned question period.

Persistent heckling needs to be dealt with strongly if it is preventing you from accomplishing your goals. You are within your rights to set a limit. For example:

> *Let's give John 2 minutes to make his comments. Then I will have to ask John to allow the rest of us to continue. If John persists in interrupting, I will have to end the presentation.* (note the flexibility and fairness of this).

Heckling can also be handled by calling an intermission (coffee break), to allow the group to address the problem by itself. This will only work if you are being attacked unfairly (from the audience's perspective) and you have acted in a dignified, fair way.

Civil objections and points should be encouraged as time allows. Allow the audience member to finish, listen carefully, and then respond by acknowledging the emotion the person has expressed. Then respond to the points as briefly as possible. If you attempt to quash dissent, you will lose the entire audience. Avoid interrupting.

Chapter Conclusions:

Dealing with audiences, either accidental ones, or companions, or doing presentations to resistant groups is a little more challenging than simple one-on-one situations, but if you can maintain your poise and self-control, and avoid getting flustered, you can then use the various techniques we've included in this book.

You will find it gets easier as you go, and you will become a bit smoother applying the techniques. You may also find that if you don't do presentations to audiences for a number of months, it will become more difficult again, and you'll have to shake off the rust. That's all normal.

Is there a bottom line to this? Perhaps. Particularly when you present to resistant groups, you must have a thick skin because it's simply impossible to please everyone in the group. Often you will be a third party coming in to speak to a group that contains at least two other factions who disagree with each other, and disagree with your message. It happens. Clearly, you can't please all the people all the time.

Chapter XVIII — Special Situations

At this point, we have presented a number of defusing tactics that will help you deal with hostile customers. There are still a few topics left to discuss. In this chapter we are going to deal with some special situations that don't fit into any of the other chapters.

THE ENVIRONMENT

The environment can play an important part in hostile interactions. We know that a shoddy, ugly and dirty environment tends to encourage lack of respect and civility. It is a good idea to take a look at the environment that the customer is seeing. Is it pleasant and comfortable? Are there reading materials for waiting customers? Is it clear where customers are expected to go? Are signs simple and clear?

 Bet You Didn't Know

Environment Matters
Sociology studies suggest that in neighborhoods where there are derelict buildings and many broken windows, poor behavior and additional damage ensues. Thus, a poorly maintained, dirty, messy or run down customer area (e.g. waiting room, store) is more likely to contribute to bad behavior on the part of customers.

TACTIC 107: PROVIDE READING MATERIAL

It's a small thing. Customers waiting for service should be provided with reading material to make their waits more bearable. What we want to do is provide something that can distract the potential angry customer from his/her anger, so that it doesn't build during a waiting period. A good selection of magazines and newspapers is easily worth the investment. More and more companies are offering short videos to waiting customers as a means of passing the time. Smart.

This also applies to your own office/cubicle. If customers visit your office, be prepared by having a newspaper and a few magazines that you can offer the client if you need to leave them for a few moments.

TACTIC 108: RE-EVALUATE YOUR ENVIRONMENT

Take a look at the environment that faces the client, from the moment she enters, to the time service is rendered. Look at it from the point of view of the client. In fact, do a "pleasantness audit". Walk through the whole process as if you have never been there. Ask yourself the following key question:

Does the environment convey that this is a place that is considerate of clients and one where the client is welcome?

Look at every detail — the way chairs are set up, size, colors, comfort, etc. If you identify things that are "user-hostile" investigate whether they can be changed. Often it isn't possible to buy entirely new furniture, but it may be possible to rearrange the furniture so people feel a bit less exposed, and more comfortable.

DEALING WITH THREATS

Luckily, the majority of threats made to employees are not carried out. BUT, it is important to treat each threat as a potential reality. Even if only one in ten thousand threats will be carried out, you don't know which ones are serious and which ones are not. Your organization should be clear about how they want you to handle threats so you need to be informed about this.

TACTIC 109: FIND OUT YOUR ORGANIZATION'S POLICY

I counsel managers to inform staff as to how they want threats handled. I also suggest that organizations develop a policy which specifies what you should do. However, you have a responsibility also. If you don't know what to do, ask your manager or supervisor. Be sure to ask what happens when you report a threat. Is it reported to the police? What action is taken, and how will you be involved in any follow-up?

If you don't have a written policy, ask for one. Don't be passive about this, since it is VERY important.

TACTIC 110: REPORT ALL THREATS

While you want to follow your organization's policy, we suggest that all threats be reported to a supervisor or manager. There should be a record of the threat, and if the manager is informed, at least he/she can take appropriate action.

Cultural Issues And Conflict

We live in a very diverse society, and our clients come to us with a wide diversity of ethnic and cultural backgrounds. Sometimes these "differences" contribute to the escalation of conflict and hostility. We are going to examine a few of the issues, without stereotyping any particular ethnic or cultural group.

PERCEPTION OF BIG BUSINESS AND GOVERNMENT

People born in other countries who have lived in other countries may have quite different perceptions of both large companies and government entities. For example a person who has lived in a country ruled by the military or a dictatorship will certainly feel different towards government than would someone raised in a democracy. It's possible people will also have differing experiences with large corporations. For example, in Japan companies play quite different roles in the lives of citizens than in North America. It's good to keep in mind that angry or frightened behavior from those coming from other nations could very well be caused by these past experiences about which we know very little. Tolerance and understanding is the order of the day, since often apparent conflict may be a result of little understood cultural differences.

COMMUNICATION/TONE OF VOICE

Different cultures have different tones of voice that are used in emotional circumstances. Some cultures are more expressive, and the tone/language makes people from these cultures sound as if they are much angrier than they seem. Try not to over-react to the tone of voice, particularly if you are dealing with someone from a different country or culture. Also be aware that your own tone of voice may mean something different than you intend and that it may be misinterpreted. If you say something in what you think is a cool professional manner, and this seems to escalate hostility, it may be useful to explore with the person whether there is misunderstanding. Ask.

INTERPERSONAL DISTANCE

Cultures (as well as individuals) vary in terms of their comfort levels with inter-personal distance. Some people (and cultures) tend to prefer conversation at a distance ... some much closer. Be aware that if you move too close, you might be perceived as confronting or preparing for attack. The best thing to do is watch the other person, since even individuals from the same culture can be different. If you see a person back away, or shrink in his chair, then back off. You got too close.

EYE CONTACT

Cultures (and individuals) vary in terms of the meaning of eye contact. Some people and cultures interpret extended eye contact as threatening while others will assume, if you don't look at them, that you are weak or aloof. Again the best guide is to observe the other person. If they look away (particularly downward), it is a good indication that your eye contact is being perceived negatively.

LANGUAGE

For people from other cultures, the words we use may be hard to understand, or worse, may be insulting. What you might see as perfectly harmless could be culturally inappropriate. In the event that you do say something that seems to upset the other person, a good approach is to ask *"Have I said something to upset you?"* and then to apologize to the person. If they attack you for the use of a word, don't defend yourself, but simply thank them for informing you that it is inappropriate.

SPECIFIC TACTICS:

Cultural differences can be complicated and difficult to deal with, and one could write complete books on the subject and still not be finished. However, consider the following:

Tactic 111: Avoid Stereotyping

Never, ever stereotype people according to ethnic background. While they may share some things in common with other people with the same heritage, they will also differ one from the other in many ways. For example, Native people from different nations, or reserves can differ as much from one another as they do from non-native people.

Tactic 112: Observe Carefully and Be Open To Learning

Look for signs of escalation or lack of understanding. Try to catch the problems early. Be prepared to look at your own behavior as part of the problem (after all, you can't be perfect). Take the opportunity to learn about the cultural group.

Tactic 113: Don't Yell

For people with English as a second language, don't yell to make yourself understood. They can hear just fine. You may want to slow down your speech slightly. A particularly good way to do this is to pause more often between sentences rather than between words.

Tactic 114: Be Patient And Understanding

Be extra patient and be aware that what you may take as common sense or common knowledge may not be so obvious to the other person. Remember that your customer is also frustrated at language and cultural differences that may be causing misunderstanding.

CAUTION!

Threats:
It may be the case that most threats are born of anger and don't translate into action, but that STILL means you need to report all threats to management according to your policy. Let professionals in the field decide what to do.

Chapter XIX — Final Comments

INTRODUCTION

By now you have probably developed a preliminary feel for both the principles of defusing hostility and the tactics you can use. Congratulations!

I would like to tell you that the hard part is behind you, but that isn't the case. The hard part isn't learning how to defuse hostility. The hard part is making effective defusing a regular habit. It's one thing to know that you shouldn't take bait, and another completely different thing to avoid taking bait. It's one thing to know a few verbal self-defense techniques and another to have them at your fingertips so you can use them smoothly and quickly.

 CAUTION!

A Starting Point
Treat this book as a starting point for learning the skills you've read about. It takes at least some effort to transfer what you've read into your life and translate it into behavior. The rewards are huge. Keep learning.

Now that you have completed this book, how are you going to keep improving at defusing hostility? That is the question you need to address. You can always get better. All of us can.

Working through this book will give you the raw material to continue getting better, provided you make a conscious effort to do so. However, you must work at it, particularly over the next few months, when you will be trying to develop and refine your skills.

How do you continue to develop? We end this book with a series of tactics you can use to continue to develop your skills.

TACTIC 115: REMIND YOURSELF

At the beginning of each working day, remind yourself of one or two defusing tactics you would like to focus upon. It might be "not taking the bait", or using a particular empathy statement, or recognizing when it is a good time to refer to a supervisor. It can be whatever you like, provided that you choose SOMETHING each day. Then mentally set a goal or two for that day in terms of using the techniques.

TACTIC 116: REVIEW PROGRESS

Since you are setting "goals" for your work days, we suggest that you take a few minutes at the end of the work day to review how you did. Did you manage to remember what you wanted to remember? If not, try again tomorrow. Nobody is perfect. If you are pleased, pat yourself on the back. Reminding yourself in the morning and reviewing in the evening need not take more than a few short minutes. After a month or two it may not be necessary to continue this practice, but it IS important at the beginning to help you continue to learn.

TACTIC 117: KEEP A HOSTILITY DIARY

If you want to be a bit more formal, you can keep a hostility diary, where you record "critical incidents" and how you handled them. In that diary you can include whatever you find useful, including daily reminders and goals, and progress you are making. This approach isn't for everyone, but you may find it useful.

TACTIC 118: DEFUSE IN YOUR PRIVATE LIFE

Many of the tactics described in this book work really well with co-workers, spouses and even children. You can gain a great deal from applying them to the rest of your life, and doing so allows you to practice a bit more. Tactics particularly useful in private life include:

- avoiding bait
- empathy statements
- listening statements
- problem solving tactics
- avoiding being triggered

Just one caution: The tactics in the verbal self-defense section can also be effective in private life, but you need to be very expert in their use, or they can backfire.

TACTIC 119: TALK TO COLLEAGUES

Your colleagues also deal with hostile people, and will have insights and ideas that you may not have considered. So, talk to your colleagues about tough situations. Consider sharing some of your experiences about what works and what doesn't. Listen, learn, and teach.

TACTIC 120: REVISIT THIS BOOK

Now that you have worked through this book, don't put it away on the shelf to be forgotten forever. Set a date, say three months from now, to reread this book. You don't have to read every single word when you go through it a second time. You may want to skim it. You may find that your second reading will give you a different slant on things. At minimum, browse the pages and read the various boxes/aids on the pages.

TACTIC 121: READ OTHER BOOKS

There are a number of books available on the topic of dealing with difficult/hostile people. Some are good, some aren't, but the more you read the more you will be able to assess the value of what you read. Read with a questioning mind.

One author that I can heartily recommend is **Suzette Haden Elgin**. She has written a series of books on verbal self-defense that I have found informative. While I do not endorse all of her suggestions, the books will give you additional knowledge and ideas that we haven't included here.

TACTIC 122: VISIT US ONLINE

We offer a variety of ways to interact with us and with other customer service staff. The best option is to go to The Customer Service Zone, our main website on...well, customer service. There you will find all kinds of amazing resources, all free. The address is http://customerservicezone.com.

We also offer a forum of sorts where you can pose customer service questions and interact with others on relevant customer service topics. The address is here in short form:

http://bit.ly/htRYKQ

While the longer address is:

http://groups.google.com/group/it-it-wasnt-for-the-customers-id-really-like-this-job

If you have any problems e-mail me at ceo@work911.com

Concluding Remarks:

In closing I want to wish you well, and good luck. My crystal ball says that customer frustration and anger isn't likely to decrease in the near future. In fact, if we continue to face economic challenges as a society, anger and stress levels will continue upwards. I believe that the ability to defuse hostility is going to be an important determinant of your job success and job satisfaction. If you couple the content of this book with your own judgment and understanding of people, you will be well off. But remember, each situation is different, and you must ultimately make the decisions that will result in good customer service and safety for all concerned.

Bacal & Associates offers bulk discounts to those that would like to order multiple copies of this workbook. If you would like a quotation for your order, contact us at the address below.

For more information about my seminars, or if you wish to share what has worked or not worked for you, you can contact me at the following address (see next page):

Robert Bacal

Bacal & Associates

722 St. Isidore Rd.

Casselman, Ontario

Canada, K0A 1M0

(613) 764-0241

Email: ceo@work911.com

Websites:

http://customerservicezone.com

http://socialmediabust.com

http://busylearners.com

CPSIA information can be obtained at www.ICGtesting.com
Printed in the USA
LVOW031510070612

285126LV00001B/19/P

9 781452 803807